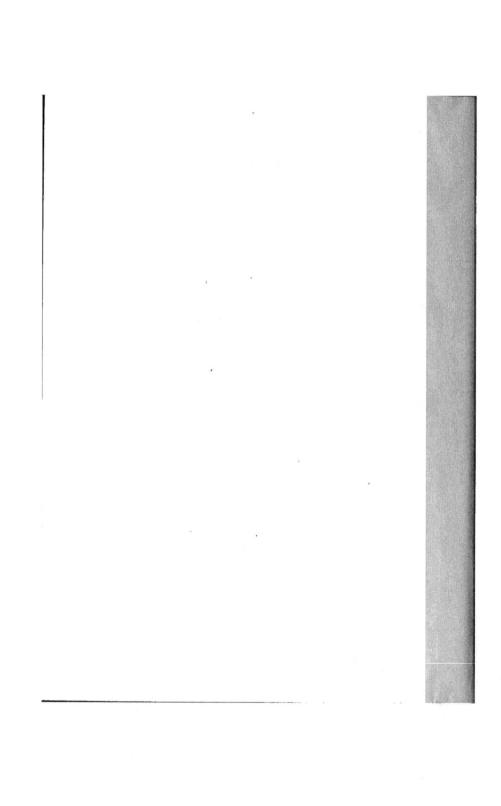

WOOLWORTH'S
FIRST 75 YEARS

THE STORY OF EVERYBODY'S STORE

1879-1954

WOOLWORTH'S
FIRST 75 YEARS

THE STORY OF EVERYBODY'S STORE

On June 21, 1879
At 170 North Queen Street, Lancaster, Pennsylvania
the Prototype of the Modern Variety Store
was opened by F. W. Woolworth

F. W. Woolworth

Frank Winfield Woolworth was born April 13, 1852, in the cottage of his paternal grandfather at Rodman, Jefferson County, New York. He was the son of John Hubbell and Fanny (McBrier) Woolworth.

When Frank was seven, his father moved the family to a farm in the township of Champion, about three-quarters of a mile from the village of Great Bend, New York. The nearest sizeable community was Watertown, the county seat, about ten miles away. In this setting, Frank Woolworth was reared, receiving a common-school education at the local schoolhouse. He also acquired an additional term of training at a Watertown commercial college.

Possessing a strong desire for merchandising, when he was about to turn 21, Woolworth found a job as stockroom boy, errand boy, janitor, general handyman, and relief clerk in Watertown's leading store, Augsbury & Moore. He was hired on a three months' trial, without pay. His hours were 7 a.m. to 9 p.m., sometimes later — an 84-hour week.

At the end of his three months' trial period, he went on the payroll at a wage of $3.50 per week. This was increased in September to $4.00, in the following March to $4.50, and by September, 1875, to $6.00. At this juncture, he was offered his choice of the head clerkship of either Augsbury & Moore or A. Bushnell's dry goods and carpet store in Watertown, the head clerks of both having resigned to form a partnership of their own. Woolworth chose the Bushnell position, at $10.00 per week — for which stipend he was required to live in the basement of the store and serve as night watchman.

After a few months, such privations took their toll and Woolworth became ill. Taking leave of absence, he returned to his father's farm. On June 11, 1876, he married Jennie Creighton, a 23-year-old seamstress from Picton, Ontario, Canada.

A year later, he returned to Watertown as senior clerk in the store of Moore & Smith, successor to Augsbury & Moore. There, Frank Woolworth helped introduce the "5¢ counter," a revolutionary new experiment in retail merchandising.

Seeing the potentialities of the new idea, Woolworth opened a "5¢ store" of his own in Utica, New York, on February 22, 1879. When this store failed after three months due to poor location, he opened a second store in Lancaster, Pennsylvania, on June 21, 1879, which proved to be a success. In 1886 his expanding business made it necessary to establish an administrative and buying office in New York City.

In 1888, strain and overwork brought on an illness which convinced Woolworth he should form an organization to carry on the business. He finally formed F. W. Woolworth & Co. in 1905. In 1912, he was joined by W. H. Moore, C. S. Woolworth, F. M. Kirby, S. H. Knox and E. P. Charlton — to form the F. W. Woolworth Co. of today. Woolworth can be said to have been the inspiration and driving force behind the new organization.

At about the same time, F. W. Woolworth also conceived and brought into being the world's first truly modern skyscraper, the Woolworth Building. He erected it with his own money, at a cost of $13,000,000 cash. It was dedicated April 24, 1913.

F. W. Woolworth served as President of the firm bearing his name from its inception until his death on April 8, 1919. (He died just five days short of his sixty-seventh birthday at his home in Glen Cove, Long Island, New York.) By that time, F. W. Woolworth Co. included 1,081 stores, in every one of the 48 states and Canada, with annual sales of $119,000,000. He was survived by his wife and two daughters, Helena and Jessie. His second daughter, Edna, had died in 1917.

F. W. WOOLWORTH CO. was formed as of January 1, 1912. It absorbed F. W. Woolworth & Co., a New York corporation; S. H. Knox & Co., a New York corporation; F. M. Kirby & Co., a Pennsylvania corporation; The E. P. Charlton & Co., a Connecticut corporation and its Canadian subsidiaries, together with the stores individually controlled by C. S. Woolworth of Scranton, Pennsylvania, W. H. Moore of Watertown, New York, and W. H. Moore & Son of Schenectady, New York.

F. W. Woolworth was the originator and innovator who laid down the principles, policies and practices on which all of these pioneers built. Contemporaries but not competitors, friendly in rivalry and in collaboration, these pioneers had all built toward a common goal.

In the lore of Woolworth's, the men pictured, together with F. W. Woolworth, collectively are known as the Founders.

F. W. Woolworth Co. is a New York corporation with principal offices in the Woolworth Building, Watertown, New York, and executive offices in the Woolworth Building, New York 7, New York. It operates in the United States and Cuba. Through a wholly-owned subsidiary, F. W. Woolworth Co., Limited, with headquarters in Toronto, the Company operates in Canada.

F. W. Woolworth Co. owns a majority of the voting shares of F. W. Woolworth & Co., Limited, with principal offices in London, operating in England, Scotland, Wales, Northern Ireland and Eire. F. W. Woolworth Co. also owns 97% of the voting shares of F. W. Woolworth Co. G. m. b. H., with principal offices in Berlin and executive offices in Frankfurt, and operating in all territories under the jurisdiction of the Bonn Government.

WILLIAM HARVEY MOORE
(1841-1916)

CHARLES SUMNER WOOLWORTH
(1856-1947)

One of the five children of Hiram and May (Salleck) Moore, W. H. Moore was born in Saratoga Springs, New York, on August 26, 1841. His father, a master mechanic of the Rome, Watertown and Ogdensburg Railroad, was a native of Stafford, Vermont. After a brief stay in Schenectady, New York, Hiram Moore brought his family to Watertown, New York, in 1853.

At the age of 15, W. H. Moore began his life-long career as a merchant at the American Corner of the Public Square in Watertown. F. W. Woolworth, C. S. Woolworth and F. M. Kirby began their mercantile careers with Mr. Moore's firm, Moore & Smith.

When Moore & Smith failed in 1885, F. W. Woolworth loaned W. H. Moore $2,000 to start a store of his own. This store was opened in the same room in which Mr. Moore had begun his career 30 years earlier. The present Woolworth Building, located on this site in Watertown, New York, houses the principal offices of F. W. Woolworth Co. and the Woolworth store that is the lineal descendant of Mr. Moore's first store. An Honorary Vice-President of F. W. Woolworth Co., Mr. Moore died in Watertown, on May 16, 1916.

Charles Sumner Woolworth was born in Rodman, Jefferson County, New York, on August 1, 1856. After a brief apprenticeship with Moore & Smith in Watertown, C. S. Woolworth became a manager for his brother, F. W. Woolworth, in Harrisburg, Pennsylvania, in 1879, and York and Scranton in 1880.

C. S. Woolworth first became the partner of F. W. Woolworth in the Scranton store, and later sole owner of that store. As a partner of F. M. Kirby, C. S. Woolworth helped to open the "Woolworth & Kirby" store in Wilkes-Barre, Pennsylvania.

C. S. Woolworth contributed importantly to the success of Woolworth's. He was a member of the original Board of Directors and of the Executive Committee, and became Chairman of the Board in 1919, following the death of F. W. Woolworth. He continued in that post until February 9, 1944, when ill health forced his retirement. C. S. Woolworth was Honorary Chairman of the Board until his death in Scranton on January 7, 1947.

His son, Richard W. Woolworth, has been a member of the Board of Directors of F. W. Woolworth Co. since his father's death.

6

O-FOUNDERS

| FRED MORGAN KIRBY | SEYMOUR HORACE KNOX | EARLE PERRY CHARLTON |
| (1861-1940) | (1861-1915) | (1863-1930) |

An only son, F. M. Kirby was born to farmer-carpenter William and Elizabeth (Slater) Kirby in Brownsville, Jefferson County, New York, on October 30, 1861. Mr. Kirby began his mercantile career with Moore & Smith in 1876, and by August, 1884, was bookkeeper and wholesale manager.

With savings of $500, and $100 borrowed from his father, F. M. Kirby became an equal partner of C. S. Woolworth in Wilkes-Barre on September 10, 1884. After purchasing C. S. Woolworth's interests on August 2, 1887, F. M. Kirby began to build his own organization. At the inception of F. W. Woolworth Co., the F. M. Kirby stores represented the third largest group.

F. M. Kirby, a man of wide interests and great philanthropies, was a tower of strength to F. W. Woolworth Co., serving as a Vice-President, a member of the Board of Directors, and on the Executive Committee from January 1, 1912 until his retirement in 1938.

F. M. Kirby died in Wilkes-Barre on October 16, 1940. Allan P. Kirby, his son, succeeded him as a member of the Board of Directors of the present F. W. Woolworth Co.

Born in Russell, New York, on April 11, 1861, S. H. Knox was the son of James and Jane (McBrier) Knox, and first cousin of F. W. and C. S. Woolworth.

In August, 1884, F. W. Woolworth invited Mr. Knox to enter into business partnership. The first "Woolworth & Knox" store, opened in Reading, Pennsylvania, on September 20, 1884, was successful. In 1886, S. H. Knox sold his interest in this store to A. H. Satterthwait. Woolworth & Knox then opened a store in Newark, New Jersey, which failed, and stores in Erie, Pennsylvania, and Lockport and Buffalo, New York, which succeeded.

F. W. Woolworth sold his interest in these stores to S. H. Knox as of December 31, 1889. S. H. Knox then formed a partnership with E. P. Charlton, which continued until December 31, 1895. Mr. Knox then proceeded to build his own organization, S. H. Knox & Co., until it was second in resources only to F. W. Woolworth & Co. at the inception of Woolworth's.

Seymour Horace Knox died in Buffalo on May 16, 1915. Seymour H. Knox of the present Board of Directors of F. W. Woolworth Co. is his son.

Son of James Duncan Charlton, blacksmith, and Lydia A. (Ladd) Charlton, and brother of Mary I. and J. Howard Charlton, E. P. Charlton was born in Chester, Connecticut, on June 19, 1863.

On February 22, 1890, in partnership with S. H. Knox, Mr. Charlton opened his first store in Fall River, Massachusetts. From then until his death on November 30, 1930, Mr. Charlton made Fall River his headquarters and home city.

Upon dissolution of his partnership with S. H. Knox on December 31, 1895, Mr. Charlton began to build his own organization. On January 1, 1899, he sold nine of his New England stores to F. W. Woolworth. With the proceeds of this sale, Mr. Charlton pioneered the Rocky Mountain and Pacific Coast States.

It is due to E. P. Charlton's pioneering that Woolworth's came into being as a truly national organization. E. P. Charlton also opened the first stores in the Western provinces of Canada.

E. P. Charlton was a Vice-President and Director of F. W. Woolworth Co. from January 1, 1912, until his death on November 30, 1930.

7

WOOLWORTH'S FIRST DECADE

	Opening Date	Location	Size of Store (ft.)	Opening Day Data			Manager January 1, 1890
				Stock	Sales	Ownership	
1879	February 22	Utica, N.Y.	14 x 25	$ 315	$ 50	F. W. Woolworth	*Failed, June, 1879*
	June 21	Lancaster, Pa.	14 x 35	410	128	F. W. Woolworth	W. D. Rock
1880	July 19	Harrisburg, Pa.	12 x 20	397	85	F. W. Woolworth	*Closed, March, 1880*
	April 3	York, Pa.	16 x 30	596	26	F. W. Woolworth	*Failed, June, 1880*
1883	November 6	Scranton, Pa.	20 x 72	625	43	F. W. Woolworth	*See note*(1)
	March 10	Philadelphia, Pa. 25¢ Store	15 x 70	1,385	46	F. W. Woolworth	*Failed, June, 1883*
1884	October 27	Lancaster, Pa.	14 x 35	948	63	F. W. Woolworth	*Failed, March, 1884*
	September 20	Reading, Pa.	16 x 45	1,531	209	F. W. Woolworth and S. H. Knox	A. H. Satterthwait
1885	October 18	Reading, Pa. 25¢ Store	14 x 125	1,900	127	F. W. Woolworth	*Failed, Dec., 1884*
	August 8	Harrisburg, Pa.	15 x 40	1,615	197	F. W. Woolworth and H. H. Hesslet	H. H. Hesslet
1886	September 5	Trenton, N.J.	15 x 90	2,192	354	F. W. Woolworth and O. Woodworth	O. Woodworth(3)
	May 15	Newark, N.J.	18 x 70	3,675	161	F. W. Woolworth and S. H. Knox	*Failed, Dec., 1886*
	August 28	Erie, Pa.	22 x 150	2,493	213	F. W. Woolworth and S. H. Knox	*See note*(2)
	October 16	Elmira, N.Y.	15 x 45	2,245	29	F. W. Woolworth and E. Northrup	E. Northrup
1887	October 23	Easton, Pa.	16 x 45	2,293	170	F. W. Woolworth and A. Getman	M. J. Getman
	September 17	Lockport, N.Y.	17 x 60	2,000	166	F. W. Woolworth and Knox, McBrier	*See note*(2)
1888	July 21	Utica, N.Y.	16 x 65	3,450	212	F. W. Woolworth and Carson C. Peck	C. C. Peck(4)
	August 11	Poughkeepsie, N.Y.	15 x 55	2,600	213	F. W. Woolworth	M. A. Creighton(5)
	September 8	Wilmington, Del.	17 x 110	2,900	216	F. W. Woolworth and B. W. Gage	B. W. Gage
	September 15	Allentown, Pa.	20 x 75	2,800	225	F. W. Woolworth and C. P. Case	C. P. Case
1889	October 13	Buffalo, N.Y.	18 x 85	4,200	261	F. W. Woolworth and S. H. Knox	*See note*(2)
	August 10	Syracuse, N.Y.	20 x 120	4,500	301	F. W. Woolworth	Mrs. A. C. Coons(5)
	October 19	New Haven, Conn.	17 x 80	4,800	315	F. W. Woolworth	A. Creighton(6)

NOTES:

1. C. S. Woolworth bought a half-interest (out of earnings) in this store in January, 1881, and the other half in January, 1883.

2. F. W. Woolworth sold his interest in these stores to S. H. Knox as of December 31, 1889.

3. F. W. Woolworth sold his interest in this store to Mr. Woodworth in 1897, and when Mr. Woodworth retired, in 1906, F. W. Woolworth & Co. (a corporation) acquired the store.

4. C. C. Peck sold his interest in this store to F. W. Woolworth as of December 31, 1889, and began his Executive Office career in New York on January 4, 1890, on a profit-sharing basis.

5. Mary Ann Creighton, F. W. Woolworth's sister-in-law, and Mrs. A. C. Coons, Woolworth's co-worker at Moore & Smith, were the first women managers of Woolworth stores.

6. Allen Creighton was F. W. Woolworth's brother-in-law.

THE FOUNDATIONS ARE LAID

Dusk was gathering after a gray and chilly Saturday afternoon on February 22, 1879. On a side street in Utica, New York, a freshly painted sign over a small shopfront proclaimed it to be the "Great 5¢ Store." Behind the store's paper-covered windows, F. W. Woolworth, proprietor, busied himself with last-minute preparations before opening for business.

A knock came at the door. Woolworth answered it. A lady, now unfortunately unidentified, held a copy of an advertising circular which the merchant had distributed that morning. She pointed to the item "fire shovels" at 5¢ each. Woolworth invited her in and wrapped up the shovel. The customer paid him 5¢ in the fractional paper currency of the day, and he promptly put it into the till.

This simple transaction marked the first sale to take place in any store owned by F. W. Woolworth, and the first from which he personally derived the profit. Thus the story of F. W. Woolworth Co. can truly be said to stem from this unobtrusively historic moment.

A month before, Frank Woolworth had been senior clerk at the Moore & Smith store, the leading retail establishment in Watertown, New York. It was there that he had helped introduce the "5¢ counter," an event which was not only to launch his own career but to revolutionize retail merchandising in the United States. The idea had caught on like wildfire, and Woolworth had watched with interest the growing success of other "5¢ counters."

At length, summoning his courage, he asked his employer, Mr. Moore, to help him set up a 5¢ store of his own, embodying the same idea. Although Moore had misgivings, he extended credit to young Woolworth for goods up to $350. The latter selected a balanced stock costing $315.41, which he left to be shipped when he found a suitable store location.

Venture in Utica

On Wednesday, February 12, 1879, F. W. Woolworth boarded a train to begin his search for a store.

He first visited Syracuse, then Rochester, Auburn, Rome and Utica. Of these, Utica, then a thriving city of 35,000, looked most promising. Woolworth located a tiny store, 14 by 25 feet, in the old Arcade Building. Although it was a little off the beaten path, its rent of $30 per month, payable at the end of the month, was within his means. Woolworth made his first commitment. Acutely aware of the slenderness of his resources and the responsibility he was under-

taking, he walked up and down the street past the telegraph office many times before finally wiring shipping instructions to Moore & Smith.

The deal for the store was closed Tuesday, February 18. By Thursday, February 20, when his stock began to arrive, Woolworth had devised fixtures of rough boards covered with cambric; had purchased such necessities as a hatchet, a box-opener and a broom; and had employed a young man, Edwins, and a young lady, Miss Stebbins, to assist him.

Thus it was that F. W. Woolworth was first launched into business on his own when the unidentified lady purchased a 5¢ fire shovel at about 6 p.m. Saturday, February 22, 1879.

Business continued brisk until 11 p.m. that night. However, as time went on, crowds did not continue to be attracted to the new 5¢ store. Although Woolworth worked from early morning until late at night, the handicap of a poor location slowly nullified all his promotional efforts. His resources were slowly being exhausted, but his faith and his determination were unabated.

Woolworth's Innovations

Many years later, Edwin Merton McBrier, a contemporary, a first cousin and partner of F. W. Woolworth, was to write the following analysis of the latter's innovations:

"The methods employed by Frank Woolworth differed from those generally used in the stores of that period. We can scarcely realize today what a decided change the Woolworth methods inaugurated. In those days the selling price of merchandise was not fixed. . . .

"On entering a dry goods store where small wares and 'Yankee Notions' were sold, one found long stretches of bare counters with clerks standing at attention behind them. . . . The stock of dry goods was carried on shelves ranged along the walls. The small wares were kept on a wide lower shelf, or in boxes under the counters. The customers were expected to make their wants known. . . . There was no such thing as 'counter display.' . . .

"Now, note the Woolworth innovations.

"First, all merchandise was to be sold *at one fixed price*. This required a new method of buying. Goods had to be purchased within certain ranges of cost in order to be sold at a fixed price and yield an average profit.

"Second, all merchandise was arranged *on the*

9

Public Square, Watertown, New York, as it appeared about 1873, when F. W. Woolworth began his mercantile career there.

counters so the purchaser could see and handle everything. This radical departure from the customary method of displaying goods was the greatest innovation of all. . . . The people were not accustomed to being invited to handle and 'see for themselves.' They came, they saw, they handled, and they bought — usually much more than they intended purchasing when they entered the store. 'Look around and see what we are selling for five cents,' the sales girls were taught to say to the customers.

"Third, it was a spot cash transaction. This also was unusual during the early years of the business. Purchasers could scarcely request credit for a few nickels' and dimes' worth of goods."

The First Successful Variety Store

By late May, when Woolworth's books showed a net worth of $252.44, he decided to leave Utica to find a new location. Leaving Edwins in charge of the Utica store, he set out for Lancaster, Pennsylvania.

The choice was a fortunate one. In 1879 Lancaster had more than 200 industrial plants and its county ranked first among all the counties in the United States in the value of its farm products per acre.

Arriving in Lancaster late Wednesday afternoon, May 28, 1879, Woolworth spent the night in a small inn and set out early next morning to search for a location. This time he kept to the busiest streets. He finally found his store at 170 North Queen Street and signed a lease at once. He was back in Utica the next day.

On Saturday, June 14, 1879, Woolworth closed the doors of his first "Great 5¢ Store." In the three months and 22 days of its existence, the store had made sales of $2,995.48 and changed Woolworth's position from debtor to a net worth of $225.88. After shipping his remaining stock and his fixtures to Lancaster, Woolworth returned to Watertown to secure more goods on credit from Moore & Smith and to pick up his family, who had remained there during his Utica venture.

Saturday, June 21, F. W. Woolworth opened his second, and Lancaster's first, "Great 5¢ Store." With a third more merchandise than at the Utica opening, seven clerks to help him instead of two, and with better displays, the opening was a spectacular success.

The next day Frank Woolworth wrote his father:

Dear Father:

I opened my store here for trade yesterday and did not advertise any. No one knew there was a 5¢ store in this city until Friday night and we managed to sell yesterday in one day $127.65, which is the most I ever sold in one day; we sold $80 in the evening alone. I had 7

10

clerks and they had to work, you bet. We could have sold $200 if the store had been larger. Jennie helped me last night. We got here Tuesday p.m. Did you get my machine all right? I want you to write and let me know all about it as soon as you get this. I think some of starting a branch store in Harrisburg, Pa. and putting Sumner in it if Moore & Smith will spare him.

F. W. Woolworth

Note that on opening day, $127.65 worth of goods were sold. The total inventory had amounted to only $410!

table on page 8 shows, many of these stores failed even as the Utica store had failed. But even more were successful, and F. W. Woolworth's faith in his fundamental principles grew firmer every day.

Harrisburg and York

Scarcely a week after he wrote his father, Woolworth was on his way to Harrisburg, about 35 miles northeast of Lancaster. On Saturday, July 19, 1879, exactly four weeks after the opening of the Lancaster store, he opened a "Great 5¢ Store" there.

Long forgotten by F. W. Woolworth but always treasured by his father, this postal card was found among the papers of John Hubbell Woolworth at his death in 1907.

It is also interesting to note that Woolworth was already planning his next branch even before the opening-day debris was swept out of his Lancaster store. His vision was firmly fixed on the principle that mass sales meant mass buying power for him. Quantity buying, in turn, meant that he could enormously expand the variety of merchandise offered under his self-imposed, uniform low selling price, and still make a profit. The key to the whole principle was more and more sales through more and more stores.

Consequently, over the next decade Woolworth opened new stores as rapidly as he could find suitable locations and the personnel to man them. As the

with his brother C. S. Woolworth as manager. Although much smaller than the Lancaster store, Harrisburg was a money-maker from the beginning.

This was apparently evident even to the landlord, for in March, 1880, he demanded an increase in rent which the little store could not support on its price structure. Unwilling to compromise with his 5¢ price, Woolworth closed the Harrisburg store, and on April 3, 1880, opened in York, Pennsylvania, with C. S. Woolworth again managing. The location at York, however, failed to produce sufficient customers and that store, too, was closed on June 30. C. S. Woolworth shipped the remaining York merchandise

F. W. Woolworth's first successful store at 170 North Queen Street, Lancaster, Pennsylvania, as it appeared in 1881.

to Lancaster and himself assumed management of the store there.

After 16 months in business for himself, F. W. Woolworth's score was: four stores opened, three closed, one thriving. But all his debts were paid and he had a net worth of $2,037.60.

The Quest for Buying Power

The answer, in part, was an important asset that did not appear on his balance sheet — buying experience. Woolworth had had to go into the market for more and more goods, first in Philadelphia, then in New York. Buying became his principal activity with his staff operating the stores. He began to buy direct from factory distributors without going through wholesalers such as Moore & Smith. He even tried to buy direct from manufacturers, and was successful at least in snapping up canceled orders and remnants of broken lines. By all these means he was able to amplify the *variety* of his stock and still make a profit at a 5¢ retail price.

It was this quest jointly for buying power and variety that led Woolworth to take a new tack. Halted temporarily in his effort to build buying power by adding new stores, he decided in the summer of 1880 to add a 10¢ line at the Lancaster store. He soon put

the bold innovation into effect. Although it did not immediately make itself felt in gross sales, doubling his top retail price instantly increased Woolworth's buying power and increased the variety of his lines fourfold. In later years, F. W. Woolworth was to rate this decision as one of the great turning points in his career.

The first "five and ten" ever opened as such was launched on Saturday, November 6, 1880, at 125 Penn Avenue, Scranton, Pennsylvania, with C. S. Woolworth as manager.

Experiments

In January, 1881, an uncle in the McBrier family offered to set up C. S. Woolworth in his own business at Cedar Springs, Michigan. Anxious to keep his brother near him, F. W. Woolworth countered with an offer of a half-interest in the Scranton store, to be paid out of earnings. Sumner accepted. Two years later, Scranton's sales were running ahead of Lancaster's, and C. S. Woolworth offered to buy out F. W. Woolworth's interest altogether. F. W. Woolworth assented.

Thus, in January, 1883, F. W. Woolworth was back where he had been on that February night in Utica four years before — a one-store operator needing variety and buying power to stay in business. But his net worth was now $9,129.13.

Woolworth embarked on two new experiments. In March, he opened his first big-city store on North Second Street, Philadelphia. In the face of disappointing sales, he closed its doors in June.

In October, he opened a 25¢ store in Lancaster. With the country going through a depression, it was soon clear that the store and the price policy were a mistake. Woolworth closed the 25¢ store in March, 1884. He was again a one-store operator.

Enter Partner-Managers

Until now, F. W. Woolworth had financed all his stores himself. The profits were all his, but so were the headaches and the heartaches. Moreover, the problem was still to build buying power and variety at a 10¢ top price. And the way to do that was to open more stores.

Therefore, Woolworth now devised a plan under which a new manager would become a partner as well by making an equal investment. Profits were *to be shared equally*. Woolworth would do all the buying and keep the general books. The partner would manage the store, send daily reports to Woolworth, and receive a nominal weekly salary to cover his necessary personal expenses.

Woolworth's first choice to launch his new policy was Seymour Horace Knox, 23, a first cousin, who was employed in H. T. M. Treglown's general store in Grand Lodge, Michigan. Each partner put in $1,000, and Knox, of course, was to manage the store. Since Knox had only $600 in savings, Woolworth loaned him the other $400, to be repaid out of profits.

Reading, Pennsylvania, was chosen for the location of the first "Woolworth & Knox" store. With opening stock valued at $1,531.47, sales on the opening day, Saturday, September 20, 1884, were $209, a new high in Woolworth's experience.

The next month, he opened his second — and last! — 25¢ store. Knox had reported that there was demand in Reading for a higher priced line. The higher price failed to return proportionate profits, however, and within ten weeks he closed the 25¢ store forever.

Woolworth now was traveling on combined buying, store-locating and partner-hunting tours. In Harrisburg, he successfully relocated in partnership with H. H. Hesslet. In Trenton, he opened in partnership with Oscar Woodworth, a glove salesman. The "Woolworth & Woodworth" store at Trenton set a new record for first-day sales and was soon the banner store of the growing group.

Moore & Smith failed early in 1885, and their stock was sold at auction. F. W. Woolworth now loaned his old friend and employer, W. H. Moore, $2,000 and

set him up in business as sole proprietor of a 5¢ and 10¢ store in the very space in which the original 5¢ counter was tried. Woolworth gave Moore every benefit of his buying and supervisory system even though he did not share in the profits.

Seymour Knox, impressed with the success of the Trenton store, came to Woolworth early in 1886 with the proposal that he move on to manage a bigger store in a larger city. They settled on Newark, New Jersey, where first-day sales totaled only $161 — and then dwindled off! Conceding failure early, the disappointed partners put a man in charge of the store and went scouting for a new location. In August of that year they opened the biggest store yet, this time in Erie, Pennsylvania. It was a resounding success, showing a profit of $3,548.96 at year-end. The partners paid off the balance of their Newark lease and closed that store.

After opening stores in October, 1886, in Elmira, New York, and Easton, Pennsylvania, both on a partner-manager basis (see table, page 8), Woolworth busied himself for almost a year with setting up a buying office and general headquarters in New York City.

A glow of satisfaction came to Woolworth in July, 1888, when he again opened a store in Utica — site of his début as a retail merchant. This time he was in a better location and had as partner-manager Carson C. Peck, an old friend from Watertown. Within 18

The pioneers posed for this picture in the backyard of F. W. Woolworth's Brooklyn home, April 29, 1889. Standing: S. H. Knox, B. W. Gage, C. S. Woolworth, F. M. Kirby, A. H. Satterthwait, Oscar Woodworth and W. D. Rock. Sitting: H. H. Hesslet, F. W. Woolworth, Mary A. Creighton, W. H. Moore.

months, Peck was to be called to a key position in Woolworth's New York headquarters.

Woolworth opened only three more stores with partner-managers. By the end of 1888, Woolworth had in training other individuals of managerial timber who lacked capital; he, on the other hand, was now in a position to supply the capital for which he formerly had to rely on partners. Hence, as the table on page 8 shows, in 1888 and 1889 he opened three stores to be operated by managers on a profit-sharing basis.

F. W. Woolworth (left) and C. S. Woolworth (right) pose with their cousin, S. H. Knox, on his wedding day in June, 1890.

The Potency of the Customer

Certain principles on which Woolworth's was to be built were emerging. As we have seen, Woolworth had early recognized the necessity for building buying power so that he could provide the widest possible *variety* of goods, at a profit, at a 10¢-top retail price. Why? Simply because only such a combination would bring customers back again and again.

Woolworth had discovered the potency of the customer. He perceived that, if he could harness the interest and buying power of the maximum number of customers, their cumulative *pull* would infinitely surpass any *push* he could put behind sales. One way to woo customers was to display goods openly. A more important way was to offer goods which the customer *wanted* to buy.

14

Woolworth came to regard himself not so much as an arbitrary buyer but rather as an agent for his customers. His habitual evaluation of a given product was in terms of *consumer satisfaction*. He realized that merchandise well-bought was almost inevitably merchandise well-sold. He also realized that, if buying power and buying responsibility were concentrated in his hands, his managers would be free to devote themselves to selling. By the same token, if he were freed of the details of selling, he could better handle the all-important task of buying.

New York Office Opened

This was the line of reasoning that led Woolworth to New York's business center in July, 1886, trying to locate suitable quarters for a permanent administrative and buying office. He finally found an office at 104 Chambers Street and had painted on the door a "Diamond W," trademark of F. W. Woolworth Co.

He immediately plunged into handling all buying, writing all orders, paying all bills, keeping the books, and writing a daily letter in longhand to his managers. The daily "General Letter" which F. W. Woolworth instituted soon after his arrival in New York served to weld the scattered stores, operated by managers of diverse personalities, into a cohesive organization and included complete data on all merchandise available to the store manager. In addition, he opened, in his own account and with others, eleven more stores in the first 41 months after establishing himself in New York. He was alone in the New York office until August, 1888, when he hired Alvin Edgar Ivie, 16, an office assistant at $6 per week. Five days later he moved his office to 280 Broadway, where it was to remain until the opening of the Woolworth Building in 1913.

Woolworth's appreciation of the importance of mass sales to build buying power implies an almost instinctive appreciation of the economic forces at work throughout this period. The period from 1880 to 1892 saw the most rapid and prolonged growth in the nation's history up to that time, particularly in manufacturing output. The same period saw a steady decline in wholesale commodity prices (see graph). Thus, with Woolworth's selling prices fixed at 5¢ and 10¢, these two factors tended constantly to broaden his buying base, to expand his lines and to widen his profit margin. Woolworth's faith and courage were founded on sound economics!

Kirby, Knox and Charlton

The same economic factors were helping shape the careers of three other merchants who were to be

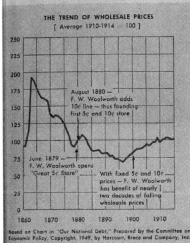

THE TREND OF WHOLESALE PRICES
[Average 1910-1914 = 100]

August 1880 —
F. W. Woolworth adds
10¢ line — thus founding
first 5¢ and 10¢ store

June 1879 —
F. W. Woolworth opens
"Great 5¢ Store"

With fixed 5¢ and 10¢
prices — F. W. Woolworth
has benefit of nearly
two decades of falling
wholesale prices

Based on Chart in "Our National Debt," Prepared by the Committee on
Economic Policy, Copyright, 1949, by Harcourt, Brace and Company, Inc.

among the Founders of F. W. Woolworth Co.: Fred Morgan Kirby, Seymour Horace Knox and Earle Perry Charlton.

In 1884, Kirby was manager of the wholesale department at Moore & Smith. On September 10 of that year he went into partnership with C. S. Woolworth, who was still operating his first store in Scranton, Pennsylvania. Together they opened a store at Wilkes-Barre. Each invested $600, Kirby's share representing not only his entire savings of $500 but $100 borrowed from his father as well. After a faltering start, the store succeeded. Three years later Kirby was able to buy out C. S. Woolworth's share and open a second store of his own in Williamsport, Pennsylvania. Eventually, F. M. Kirby operated a total of 96 successful stores.

Kirby adhered strictly to the policy of building from within, a policy which in 1954 still is fundamental in the operation of F. W. Woolworth Co.

F. M. Kirby also inspired great personal loyalty. He loyally served his managers, his employees, and the communities in which he operated his stores, and they reciprocated his loyalty to them. His first store in Wilkes-Barre, Pennsylvania, still bears his name, although it is an integral part of F. W. Woolworth Co. F. M. Kirby's contribution of 96 successful stores to the formation of F. W. Woolworth Co. was important not only in terms of numbers, but in terms of net profits, and of locations. Particularly, F. M. Kirby may be given credit for opening and developing the South.

Seymour Knox, in January, 1890, purchased F. W. Woolworth's interests in the Erie, Buffalo and Lockport stores and embarked on his own business enterprise. Twenty-one years later, he was operating 112 stores.

E. P. Charlton entered the picture as partner with S. H. Knox in a store in Fall River, Massachusetts, which opened in February, 1890, and still bears his name. Six years later, he too, started his own organization. By 1911 he was operating 53 stores.

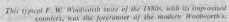

This typical F. W. Woolworth store of the 1880s, with its improvised counters, was the forerunner of the modern Woolworth's.

F. W. Woolworth's first New York store, opened in 1895, as it appeared in 1897. The diorama from which this picture was made is a permanent exhibit at The Museum of the City of New York.

Organization

Late in 1888, F. W. Woolworth suffered an illness which was to affect profoundly his theories of business organization. Strain and overwork took their toll. His weight dropped to an alarming 135 pounds. Finally he fell victim of typhoid fever and collapsed. He remained in bed about nine weeks.

F. W. Woolworth was to recall later, "After that [illness], I contented myself with the important matters, planning for expansion and a general oversight of the business, placing responsibility for execution of details upon my associates. . . . As soon as a business grows beyond one's ability to attend to all the details himself, he must trust to organization and cooperation to carry it forward." In short, Woolworth's illness had taught him to "organize, deputize, supervise."

Highly significant evidence of this change was contained in a General Letter to his managers dated October 11, 1889. In it, Woolworth said:

"I have had under consideration for some time, the formation of a stock company. . . .

"There are 35 cities east of the Rocky Mountains that have a population of over 50,000 people in which we do not have stores. There are a large number of cities between 20,000 and 50,000 in which we do not have stores in which our business would be sure of success. . . .

"My idea would be, after the company was organized, to open up stores in these cities, perhaps ten or twelve per year. In order to do that, we must have one or two men to look up good locations, rent each such store, make the contract for fitting it up and simply send his order to the New York office to ship complete stock to that point. Another man would follow to open up the goods, employ help and stay there until the store was opened a week or more and

then leave it in charge of the man appointed to take charge of it permanently. So much for the new stores.

"Now my idea would be to have a man make it a business to visit the old stores, continually, and give them points on all new goods, new prices, new ways to display goods, and a thousand things that would come up. So much for outside work.

"In the New York office, it would be necessary to have a good man to be responsible for the finances of the company, to take charge of the employees in the office and see that the books are properly kept and that reports are made out correctly. Last but not least, there would be competent buyers there.

"All New York office expenses would have to be borne by the company which would be quite a large expense. . . .

"For the first year, we would have all goods shipped direct to stores, but after that, we might carry stock in a warehouse in New York of some of the small goods that we could buy to good advantage in large quantities. . . ."

Thus, his mind working restlessly as he recuperated from his long illness, F. W. Woolworth forged the rough plan that was to culminate 23 years later in the organization of F. W. Woolworth Co.

The Era of Growth

The scene is again a Woolworth store in Utica, New York. Again it is near the end of a chill and gray winter afternoon. Carson C. Peck, until recently partner-manager of the Utica store, completed turning over the business records to his successor, bade good-bye to the staff, and walked out the front door. On January 4, 1890, he reported to F. W. Woolworth's New York Executive Office, the first manager to serve in the central organization on a profit-sharing basis. Peck's move was symbolic of the vast and

16

stirring changes that were to take place in the Woolworth organization over the next two decades.

The threefold means by which this astonishing growth (see accompanying table) was brought about were all established in the crucial decades, 1890-1910.

First, Woolworth established a central organization in New York City to do the buying, handle the financial and administrative duties, and supervise field operations.

Secondly, he built an organization among his retail stores from which he could draw constantly for new managerial talent. At the same time, he crystallized certain vital personnel policies for retail help.

Thirdly, he carried on a ceaseless program of acquiring stores owned either wholly or in part by others and of opening new stores of his own. Simultaneously, he expanded and improved his existing stores.

F. W. WOOLWORTH'S FIRST 30 YEARS			
(As of December 31)			
Year	Number of Stores in Operation	Gross Sales (Year)	Net Worth
1879	2	$ 12,024	$ 1,517
1889	12	246,782	68,376
1899	54	4,415,111	875,000
1909	238	23,317,807	6,186,944

Until the arrival of Carson C. Peck in January, 1890, F. W. Woolworth *was* the New York Executive Office. Peck was immediately assigned buying duties and the supervision of "learners," as embryo-managers were, and still are, called. Two years later, in April, 1892, H. T. Parson was added to the staff, the first career financial man in the organization. Peck was to become a master merchandiser, able administrator, and superb handler of men; Parson, the efficient handler of records and money matters.

By 1900, additional staff members had been added. H. A. Moody, E. C. Webb and C. M. Osborn were buyers of American-made merchandise. C. P. Case was buyer of imported goods, making semi-annual trips to Europe. He was later to become supervisor of buyers and Peck's able assistant. B. W. Gage, superintendent of construction, was the brilliant planner and designer of stores who did much to develop the standards of efficiency, convenience, safety and

sanitation that mark the modern variety store. In addition to these staff members, the Executive Office employed five stenographers, nine male bookkeepers, one mimeograph operator and one office girl.

As soon as Carson C. Peck was installed in the New York office, Woolworth began preparations for his first buying trip to Europe. He sailed on February 19, 1890.

Even prior to 1890, Woolworth had begun a program of encouraging American manufacturers to produce needed items for his stores and, where necessary, placing initial orders large enough to warrant a factory change-over. His foresight was indeed providential, for by the end of 1896 (as shown in the graph, page 15) the downward trend of two decades was reversed and the wholesale cost of goods began to rise. Since his selling prices were fixed, this meant that Woolworth's profit margin was narrowed.

Development from Within

At the time this development was taking place in New York, Woolworth was building a strong field organization. He adhered strictly to the policy of developing managerial ability from within, rather than hiring it on the outside. At the base of the organizational pyramid were the "learners," promising young men who started in the stockroom, even as Woolworth and Peck had, and who were put through an intensive training program. When a manager for a new store was needed, the assistant manager of an existing store was promoted to the new position, and a "learner" was moved into the latter's place. When the number of stores grew too large to be supervised from New York, a manager was promoted to become a supervisor of stores. When the number of supervisors, in turn, became too large for centralized control, a District Office was created, and a supervisor of stores was promoted to District Manager, starting another chain-reaction of advancements all the way down the line.

Until 1898, F. W. Woolworth personally supervised all his stores, usually by unannounced visits of inspection. In that year, C. C. Griswold was appointed first supervisor of stores, and a second supervisor was appointed within two years. Griswold became the first District Manager, in Chicago, in 1904. Over the next four years, six other District Offices were opened, and by 1910, eight.

As F. W. Woolworth valued close personal acquaintanceship with members of his organization, it was a source of regret to him when continued expansion made it impossible to keep in close touch. In their Lancaster days, the Woolworths customarily had their employees in for Sunday tea. In Brooklyn,

17

Woolworth's home was open to his managers on their visits to New York, and the first convention of managers was held there in 1889. Soon, however, a summer resort or hotel was needed to house conventions of managers. Further growth necessitated district conventions, which removed personal contact another step.

Policies Are Born

Ever since profit-sharing managers had been established in the Woolworth organization, the manager set the salaries for his employees and the learners assigned to him. In the 1890s, F. W. Woolworth began to set minimum wages for employees at all levels of operation, but left the top limits to the manager. His General Letters clearly show that Woolworth was constantly urging his managers to pay *more* to competent employees as they assumed larger responsibilities. Woolworth instituted paid vacations for employees in 1895, and Christmas bonuses in 1897.

With the upturn of wholesale prices, it became all the more important for F. W. Woolworth to harness an ever increasing share of the buying power of the market by acquiring more and more stores. In 1899, he bought nine stores from E. P. Charlton. His experience in assimilating the Charlton stores was put to good use in succeeding years. In February and March, 1904, for example, Woolworth, with the help of C. C. Griswold, in 22 days inspected and purchased 21 stores of Pfohl, Smith & Co. and three other operators in the Mid-West. For these properties, Woolworth paid more than $500,000 cash. In August, he bought 12 stores from G. C. Murphy in Pennsylvania, and the next month, three from E. H. Farnsworth in New England.

Expansion and Modernization

As these acquisitions were being made, F. W. Woolworth continued opening stores of his own. In 1895 he opened his first successful "big-city" store, in Brooklyn. He may have been influenced by observing the success of a store opened the year before by S. H. Knox in the finest shopping neighborhood in Detroit. De luxe in every appointment, the Knox store was an immediate hit. Woolworth's Brooklyn unit was also such a resounding success that he opened two more "big-city" stores within a year, one in Boston, the other on Sixth Avenue, New York.

While Woolworth's main new-store program continued to be concentrated in the smaller agricultural-industrial cities, he initiated a concurrent program to expand and modernize existing stores. For example, until 1900 cash was conveyed by cable conveyors in all stores. After a test in that year, cash registers became standard equipment. At about the same time, mirrored walls and glass display shelves began to replace the old wooden shelves back of the counters.

The other Founders were also actively expanding their organizations in this same period. S. H. Knox made a spectacular advance in 1904. A friend of his, John Seibert, had started a variety store business in the West with a partner, Daniel Good. Seibert was now retired because of ill health and Good offered to merge the 22 stores of Seibert, Good & Co. with the Knox group. This was accomplished with the incorporation of S. H. Knox & Co. on February 24, 1904.

F. W. Woolworth & Co.

The "stock company" which F. W. Woolworth first proposed in his General Letter in 1889 became a reality on February 16, 1905. F. W. Woolworth & Co. was incorporated in the State of New York with principal offices in Mineola, New York, and executive offices at 280 Broadway, New York City. Authorized capitalization was $10,000,000, represented by equal amounts of 7% cumulative preferred and common stocks.

The first Board of Directors of F. W. Woolworth & Co. consisted of: F. W. Woolworth, President; Carson C. Peck, Vice-President and General Manager; C. P. Case, Vice-President; H. T. Parson, Secretary-Treasurer; and H. A. Moody. (All except Parson had begun their careers in Watertown!) Other officers included C. C. Griswold and H. W. Cowan, Assistant Treasurers.

In his fifty-eighth year, F. W. Woolworth embarked on one of the great ventures of his career. He sailed for England on May 19, 1909 to launch F. W. Woolworth & Co., Limited. Fred M. Woolworth, a third cousin of F. W. Woolworth, B. D. Miller and S. R. Balfour formed the American nucleus of the new company which was to operate in England, Scotland, Wales, Northern Ireland and Eire. Miller returned to the United States in 1920 to become first a Vice-President and later President of F. W. Woolworth Co. William L. Stephenson, the first Englishman to be hired by the new company, eventually succeeded Fred M. Woolworth as Managing Director of F. W. Woolworth & Co., Limited, upon the latter's death in 1923. By the end of 1910, F. W. Woolworth & Co., Limited (England) was, like its parent, F. W. Woolworth & Co., a resounding success. The people of England had welcomed Woolworth's values as enthusiastically as had the people of the United States.

The stage was now set for Frank Winfield Woolworth's greatest achievement: the formation of the F. W. Woolworth Co. of today.

18

Progress! — A horse-car passes in the foreground as the Woolworth Building rises in the background. Time; 1912.

The Woolworth Building in New York endures as F. W. Woolworth's personal monument. In Woolworth's lifetime, he was the owner of the building, and since his death the building has been owned by a successor corporation. F. W. Woolworth Co. has been a regular rent-paying tenant of the Woolworth Building since 1913.

BUILDING FOR TOMORROW

F. W. Woolworth lived in the era of the horse-car, but he planned and built for the future.

F. W. Woolworth's great and enduring monument stands as a living witness of his genius for working cooperatively and productively with and through others. Only the collaboration of his Co-Founders made it possible for F. W. Woolworth to lay the broad foundation, and only the skill and industry of the successors of the Founders in ownership and management made possible the building of his living and lasting monument, today's F. W. Woolworth Co.

The story of the people who have built F. W. Woolworth Co. into the great enterprise it is today is told in the pages that follow.

19

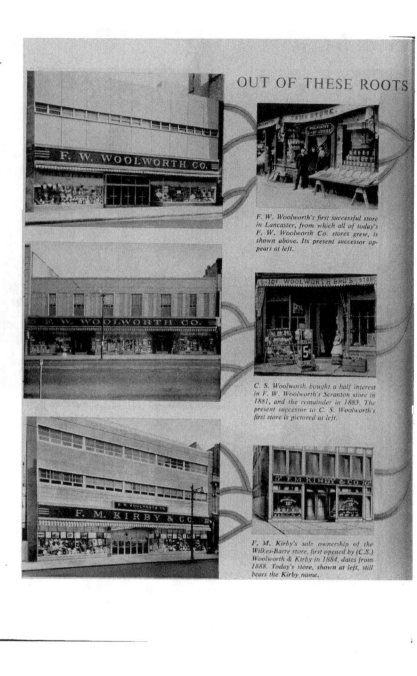

F. W. Woolworth's first successful store in Lancaster, from which all of today's F. W. Woolworth Co. stores grew, is shown above. Its present successor appears at left.

C. S. Woolworth bought a half interest in F. W. Woolworth's Scranton store in 1881, and the remainder in 1883. The present successor to C. S. Woolworth's first store is pictured at left.

F. M. Kirby's sole ownership of the Wilkes-Barre store, first opened by (C.S.) Woolworth & Kirby in 1884, dates from 1888. Today's store, shown at left, still bears the Kirby name.

F. W. WOOLWORTH CO.

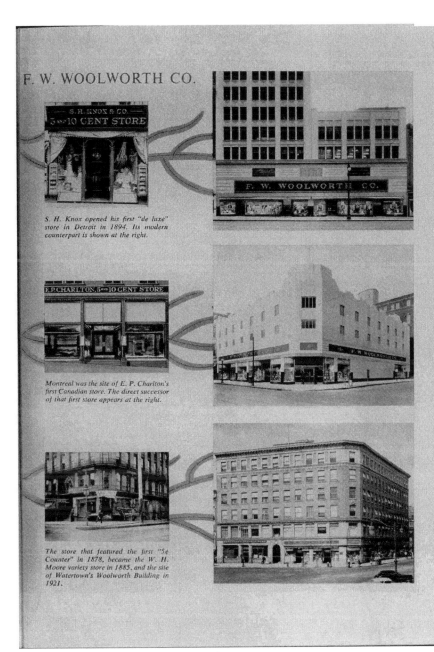

S. H. Knox opened his first "de luxe" store in Detroit in 1894. Its modern counterpart is shown at the right.

Montreal was the site of E. P. Charlton's first Canadian store. The direct successor of that first store appears at the right.

The store that featured the first "5¢ Counter" in 1878, became the W. H. Moore variety store in 1885, and the site of Watertown's Woolworth Building in 1921.

$6,000,000

F. W. Woolworth Co.

Incorporated under the laws of the State of New York

Seven Per Cent. Cumulative Preferred Stock

Preferred as to dividends and as to assets in liquidation.

The whole or any part redeemable at the option of the Company on three months' notice, at 125%, and accrued dividends

Dividends Payable Quarterly April, July, October and January

Par Value of Shares $100

Farmers' Loan & Trust Co., New York, N. Y.
Transfer Agent

Lawyers' Title Insurance & Trust Co., New York, N. Y.
Registrar

CAPITALIZATION

Seven Per Cent. Cumulative Preferred Stock,
Dividends payable quarterly beginning April 1st, 1912:
Authorized and Issued $15,000,000

Common Stock:
Authorized and Issued $50,000,000

F. W. Woolworth Co. was organized under the laws of the State of New York to take over as going concerns the following businesses:

(1) F. W. Woolworth & Co., a New York Corporation.
(2) S. H. Knox & Co., a New York Corporation.
(3) F. M. Kirby & Co., a Pennsylvania Corporation.
(4) The E. P. Charlton & Co., a Connecticut Corporation.
(5) The five and ten cent store business of C. S. Woolworth.
(6) The five and ten cent store businesses of W. H. Moore and W. H. Moore & Son.
(7) The controlling interest in F. W. Woolworth & Co., Ltd., owned by F. W. Woolworth & Co., and now operating 12 stores in England.

The undersigned are in receipt of a letter from Mr. F. W. Woolworth, President of the Company, which is hereto attached, with respect to the purposes of the merger and the history of the businesses of the above-mentioned Companies. The following is the balance sheet and statement of earnings of the Companies included in the merger, which has been furnished us by Messrs. Touche, Niven & Co., Chartered Accountants.

F. W. Woolworth Co.

(Incorporated 15th December 1911.)

Initial Balance Sheet

Introducing Assets and Liabilities, to be taken over as of the date of January 1st, 1912, of F. W. Woolworth & Co., S. H. Knox & Co., F. M. Kirby & Co., The E. P. Charlton & Co., C. S. Woolworth, W. H. Moore and W. H. Moore & Son, and Assets and Liabilities of the Subsidiary Corporations of the four first named Companies.

ASSETS			LIABILITIES		
Leases, Alterations and Improvements, Furniture and Fixtures and Goodwill		$55,009,387.87	Capital Stock to be Authorized and Issued:		
Real Estate		607,751.15	7% Cumulative Preferred Stock 150,000 Shares of $100.00 each	$15,000,000.00	
Investments:			Common 500,000 Shares of $100.00 each	50,000,000.00	
F. W. Woolworth & Co., Ltd., England	$279,928.41			$65,000,000.00	
Real Estate Mortgage	30,000.00	309,928.41	Purchase Money Mortgages on Real Estate		30,000.00
Inventories of Merchandise		8,141,069.75	Sundry Creditors		52,154.68
Supplies and Prepaid Expenses		160,727.30	Reserve for Federal Corporation Tax and Miscellaneous Taxes		75,000.00
Sundry Debtors		101,047.43			
Cash in Banks and on Hand		827,302.77			
		$65,157,154.68			$65,157,154.68

New York, February 7th, 1912. We certify that the foregoing is a correct statement of the Assets and Liabilities of F. W. Woolworth Co., as the same will appear upon the completion of the organization of the Company

We have further examined the Accounts of F. W. Woolworth & Co., S. H. Knox & Co., F. M. Kirby & Co., The E. P. Charlton & Co., C. S. Woolworth, W. H. Moore, and W. H. Moore & Son, the undertakings of which F. W. Woolworth Co. is to acquire, for the six calendar years ending December 31st, 1911, and certify that the combined Sales and Profits of the Merged Businesses have been as follows:

		SALES	PROFITS
Year 1906	· · ·	$27,760,664.07	$2,723,354.22
Year 1907	· · ·	32,968,144.84	2,971,118.99
Year 1908	· · ·	36,206,674.24	3,617,077.15
Year 1909	· · ·	44,438,193.39	4,702,802.23
Year 1910	· · ·	50,841,546.98	5,065,031.04
Year 1911	· · ·	52,616,123.68	4,955,255.57

(Signed) TOUCHE, NIVEN & CO., New York.
GEORGE A. TOUCHE & CO., London,
Chartered Accountants.

THE LETTER FROM MR. F. W. WOOLWORTH, PRESIDENT, HEREINBEFORE REFERRED TO, WITH
RESPECT TO THE PURPOSES OF THE MERGER AND THE HISTORY AND BUSINESS OF THE COMPANY:

New York, N. Y., February 14, 1912.

MESSRS. GOLDMAN, SACHS & CO. AND LEHMAN BROTHERS,
  NEW YORK CITY, N. Y., AND
MESSRS. KLEINWORT, SONS & CO.,
  LONDON, ENGLAND.

DEAR SIRS:

Referring to the purchase by you of 60,000 shares of the Seven Per Cent. Cumulative Preferred
Stock of the F. W. Woolworth Co., incorporated December 15th, 1911, under the laws of the State of
New York, I beg to say for myself and as President:

Capitalization

The Company has no mortgage or funded indebtedness, the capitalization being as follows:
7% Cumulative Preferred Stock:
  Authorized and issued   -   -   -   - $15,000,000.
Common Stock,
  Authorized and issued   50,000,000.

Purpose of Formation

F. W. Woolworth Co. was formed for the purpose of acquiring the businesses of:
F. W. Woolworth & Co., a New York Corporation.
S. H. Knox & Co., a New York Corporation.
F. M. Kirby & Co., a Pennsylvania Corporation.
The E. P. Charlton & Co., a Connecticut Corporation.
The "5 and 10 Cent" store business of C. S. Woolworth.
The "5 and 10 Cent" store businesses of W. H. Moore and W. H. Moore & Son.
The controlling interest of F. W. Woolworth & Co. in F. W. Woolworth & Co., Ltd., of
  Great Britain.

These companies have never in any way been competitors in the sale of goods nor has any of them
maintained or operated a store in any city or town in which any other of said companies has maintained
or operated a store.

History

The businesses acquired have been engaged in the operation of so-called "5 and 10 Cent" stores
in different sections of the United States, Canada and England.

This class of business was originally started in Lancaster, Pennsylvania, in 1879, and has steadily
grown, until at the present time, the new F. W. Woolworth Co. operates or controls about 558 stores in
the United States and 32 stores in Canada, and owns a controlling interest in F. W. Woolworth & Co.
Ltd., of Great Britain, operating thus far twelve stores in England.

We employ about 20,000 people and cater to about three million customers a day. Our business
is conducted on a strictly cash basis, so that there are no losses entailed by bad accounts. The success
of our organization may be attributed to a great buying power and ability to take advantage of all cash
discounts, combined with economy in distribution.

The popularity of the business is unquestioned and is evidenced by its remarkable growth, which
has been unusually steady and of a healthy character. From its inception the business has grown
annually even in the face of occasional panics and hard times.

Sales and Earnings

The gross sales and net profits of the combined stores for the six years ending Dec. 31st., 1911
have been as follows:

	SALES	PROFITS
Year 1906	$27,760,664.07	$2,723,354.22
Year 1907	32,968,144.84	2,971,118.99
Year 1908	36,206,674.24	3,617,077.15
Year 1909	44,438,193.39	4,742,802.23
Year 1910	50,841,546.98	5,065,031.64
Year 1911	52,616,123.68	4,955,255.57

The net profits for the past three years are equal to an average of almost five times the annual
dividend on the 7% Cumulative Preferred Stock, or at the rate of over 7⅜% per annum on the Common
Stock.

Future Possibilities

I believe the business is still in its infancy and capable under the new organization of great future
development. The management of the new company will include those gentlemen in whose hands the
acquired businesses have achieved success in the past. In my judgement, however, the organization of
the company has been so perfected as to render the conduct and further development of the business independent of the individuality of any one person.

Yours very truly,

(Signed) F. W. WOOLWORTH.

F. W. WOOLWORTH CO.
MERGED BUSINESSES.
COMBINED BALANCE SHEET, DECEMBER 31, 1911.

	F.W.Woolworth & Co.	S. H. Knox & Co.	F. M. Kirby & Co.	The E. P. Charlton & Co.	C. S. Woolworth.	W. H. Moore and W. H. Moore & Son	Total
ASSETS.							
Good-will	$7,500,000.00	$2,521,410.00	$3,631,292.18	$1,500,000.00	....	....	$15,453,102.18
Alterations and improvements	621,440.89	517,072.93	326,921.93	193,569.52	$6,987.49	$2,371.78	1,578,284.54
Furniture and fixtures	1,784,265.45	600,733.36	525,271.44	369,218.74	65,905.60	19,709.49	3,356,103.93
Real estate	466,039.86	113,861.29	25,000.00	850.00	....	....	607,751.15
Investments:							
F. W. Woolworth & Co., Ltd., England	279,928.41	....	....	....	....	....	279,928.41
Real estate mortgage		30,000.00	....	....	....	....	30,000.00
Inventories of merchandise	4,570,293.95	1,502,328.61	1,167,602.93	659,349.60	203,113.79	38,319.87	8,141,009.75
Supplies and prepaid expenses	86,230.82	30,062.01	27,464.29	13,072.13	2,935.99	561.96	160,727.20
Sundry debtors	44,593.23	17,129.43	20,739.44	17,985.33	528.78	70.22	101,047.43
Cash in banks and on hand	607,214.58	56,310.58	34,953.81	296,118.85	32,114.82	6,584.18	1,034,296.82
Total assets	$15,962,007.19	$5,689,308.15	$5,759,647.12	$2,960,164.17	$312,506.87	$8,617.41	$30,742,250.91
LIABILITIES.							
Sundry creditors	$15,155.36	$1,820.24	$20,164.19	$14,404.41	$200.97	$439.51	$52,154.68
Real estate mortgage	30,000.00	....	....	....	....	....	30,000.00
Capital Stock, capital and surplus	15,916,821.83	5,687,487.91	5,739,542.93	2,945,759.76	312,305.90	58,177.90	30,560,096.23
	$15,962,007.19	$5,689,308.15	$5,759,647.12	$2,960,164.17	$312,506.87	$58,617.41	$30,742,250.91

The table above is a photographic reproduction of one appearing in the application for listing of the Common Stock of F. W. Woolworth Co. on the New York Stock Exchange, June 26, 1912. The $15,000,000 Preferred Stock also listed at that time represents the tangible assets of the new company. The $50,000,000 Common Stock represents intangibles. Besides "Good Will," the "intangibles" contributed by the Founding Fathers were those shown in the other tables on this page.

EXPERIENCED EXECUTIVE OPERATION

Contributed by the Merged Businesses	Officers, Directors, District Managers	Executive Office Buyers Plus 1 Fixtures Superintendent	District Office Personnel Other Than District Manager	Total	% of Total
F. W. Woolworth & Co.	8	9	21	38	49%
S. H. Knox & Co.	4	3	9	16	21
F. M. Kirby & Co.	2	5	5	12	15
The E. P. Charlton & Co.	2	2	5	9	12
C. S. Woolworth	1		2	3	3
TOTAL	17	19	42	78	100%

EXPERIENCED EXECUTIVE DIRECTION

EXECUTIVE COMMITTEE

Carson C. Peck, *Chairman*

F. W. Woolworth

S. H. Knox

F. M. Kirby

E. P. Charlton

C. S. Woolworth

H. T. Parson

WELL-MANAGED, WIDELY-DISTRIBUTED, PROFITABLE STORES

Merged Businesses	Sales for Calendar Year 1911	Stores in Operation January 1, 1912		
		United States*	Canada	Totals
F. W. Woolworth & Co.	$26,887,035	319		319
S. H. Knox & Co.	13,047,745	98	13	111
F. M. Kirby & Co.	7,253,036	96		96
The E. P. Charlton & Co.	4,070,683	35	18	53
C. S. Woolworth	1,207,849	15		15
W. H. Moore	149,776	2		2
TOTALS	$52,616,124	565	31	596**

* These stores were located in 37 of the 46 states, and the District of Columbia.
** Includes stores under construction and opened for business during 1912.

The INVESTOR:
Successor in Ownership to the Founders

F. W. Woolworth Co. came into being by the simple exchange of all of its capital stock for all of the capital 'stocks of F. W. Woolworth & Co., S. H. Knox & Co., F. M. Kirby & Co., and The E. P. Charlton & Co., and for the assets of C. S. Woolworth, W. H. Moore and W. H. Moore & Son.

By this transaction, however, no public market for the stock of F. W. Woolworth Co. was established. The Founders, therefore, chose to offer to the public through bankers $6,000,000 par value of a total of $15,000,000 of Preferred Stock and $7,000,000 par value of a total of $50,000,000 of Common Stock, apportioned according to their holdings. While they agreed not to dispose of any of their other stock for one year, they reserved the right to distribute $1,500,000 par value of either Preferred or Common stock to employees of the new company.

Employee Participation

The shares thus set aside were offered to store managers and executives at $50 per share for the Common and $100 for the Preferred. Subscriptions were received from the managers of 217 stores.

In a General Letter issued in connection with such an offering, Carson C. Peck said in part: ". . . You have an absolutely sure 6% investment and you don't want to fret . . . if the stock should drop 10, 15, yes, 20 points per share. Hang on to it. . . . On the other hand, don't get excited if you see the stock go up a few points per share. I say, keep it! Don't sell it any more than you would sell your birthright."

By February 1, 1923, all of the Preferred Stock had been retired at $125 per share. By the end of 1925, the $50,000,000 item of "Good Will" (included in the first item of the Balance Sheet in the original Offering Circular) had been written off to a nominal $1, reflecting the sound growth and stability of the Company.

Public Participation

Every investor now holding the Common Stock of F. W. Woolworth Co. is the successor in ownership of one of the Founders. Since the incorporation, the Company has never made a public offering of its securities. The growth of the Company has come entirely from retained earnings. Retained earnings also made possible the retirement of the $15,000,000 par value of Preferred Stock originally issued, and the write-down of the "Good Will" account to $1. Yet F. W. Woolworth Co. has paid a dividend every year since its inception as of January 1, 1912.

Although F. W. Woolworth Co. stock originally was offered to the public February 19, 1912, it had actually been traded on a "when issued" basis on the New York Curb, predecessor of the American Stock Exchange, since the preliminary announcement of the offering three months before. The bankers set a price of 101½ on the Preferred and 55 on the Common for the public offering. As evidenced below, the investing public put a value of 109 on the Preferred and 80¾ on the Common in the open market on the day of the offering.

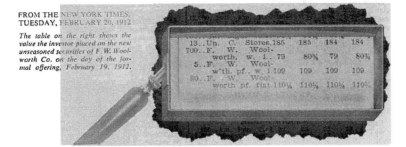

FROM THE NEW YORK TIMES, TUESDAY, FEBRUARY 20, 1912

The table on the right shows the value the investor placed on the new unseasoned securities of F. W. Woolworth Co. on the day of the formal offering, February 19, 1912.

13	Un.	C.	Stores.	185	185	184	184
700	F.	W.	Woolworth,	w. i.	79	80¾	79	80¾
5	F.	W.	Woolw'th. pf. w. i	109	109	109	109
80	F.	W.	Woolworth pf. flat.	110¼	110¼	110¼	110¾

The concluding paragraph of F. W. Woolworth's prophetic letter of 1912, reproduced in the Offering Circular, sets forth three distinct points, all of which have been borne out by later events. This is especially true of the statement ". . . further development of the business [is] independent of the individuality of any one person."

Nevertheless, after F. W. Woolworth himself, the personality of Carson C. Peck remains unique in *Woolworth's First 75 Years.* From 1890 onward, Mr. Peck built into the Woolworth organization the flexibility and dynamism that made it possible in 1912 to unite the separate organizations of the Founders, in a matter of months.

At the inception of F. W. Woolworth Co., Carson C. Peck was Director, Vice-President, General Manager and Chairman of the Executive Committee. In the formative years, until his death on April 29, 1915, Mr. Peck was active head of the Company. During much of this period Mr. Woolworth was gravely ill. Mr. Peck's last full year of activity was 1914. By then F. W. Woolworth Co. had been built from six separate organizations, operating 596 stores, with aggregate sales of $52 millions into one organization with 737 stores and sales of $69 millions.

F. W. Woolworth resumed active management of the Company on the death of Mr. Peck. Of 48 subsequent monthly meetings of the Board of Directors, up to the date of his own death in 1919, F. W. Woolworth attended all but five. C. C. Griswold succeeded C. C. Peck as General Manager, but Mr. Griswold himself died on January 27, 1916. Upon the death of Mr. Griswold, H. T. Parson was elected Vice-President and General Manager.

The principles of organization molded and inspired by Carson C. Peck in the formative years of F. W. Woolworth Co. continue to function as the Company concludes its first 75 years.

CARSON C. PECK
(1858-1915)

HUBERT T. PARSON
(1872-1940)

Carson C. Peck was born in Stone Mills, Jefferson County, New York, on January 10, 1858. He began his mercantile career with A. Bushnell, Watertown, New York, in 1876, shortly after Woolworth, his friend, returned to the farm due to illness. Mr. Woolworth kept in constant touch with him and on July 21, 1888, Mr. Peck became his partner-manager in Utica, New York.

Mr. Peck soon demonstrated the talents and capacities Mr. Woolworth was seeking in order to implement his plans for building his expanding organization around a strong central executive staff. On December 31, 1889, Mr. Woolworth bought Mr. Peck's interest in the Utica store, and brought him to New York as a "manager-buyer," under a profit-sharing arrangement. Thereafter, Mr. Peck was the practical merchandiser, the able financial organizer, the trainer of managers, that Mr. Woolworth needed to make his plans work.

On April 29, 1915, Carson C. Peck died in Brooklyn, his adopted home town since 1890. He was buried in the family plot at Watertown, New York. His son, Fremont C. Peck, is a member of the Board of Directors of F. W. Woolworth Co.

Born in Toronto, Canada, on September 10, 1872, Hubert T. Parson was educated in Brooklyn. He became F. W. Woolworth's first bookkeeper in 1892. When F. W. Woolworth & Co. was incorporated in 1905, Mr. Parson was elected a Director and Secretary-Treasurer.

At the formation of F. W. Woolworth Co., Mr. Parson was elected Director, member of the Executive Committee, and Secretary. At the death of C. C. Griswold in 1916, he became Vice-President and General Manager.

Upon the death of F. W. Woolworth on April 8, 1919, H. T. Parson became President, serving under C. S. Woolworth, who became the first Chairman of the Board at the same time.

In 1919, Mr. Parson's first year as President, F. W. Woolworth Co. operated 1,081 stores with sales of $119 millions. In 1931, the last full year of his active career, sales of 1,903 Woolworth's stores aggregated $282 millions. Meanwhile, F. W. Woolworth Co. had opened its first store in Cuba in 1924, and in Germany in 1927.

Hubert T. Parson retired as President in 1932, but remained a Director until 1938. He died on July 9, 1940.

BYRON D. MILLER

CHARLES W. DEYO
(1880-1952)

ALFRED L. CORNWELL

Byron D. Miller, Woolworth's third President, still is a member of the Board of Directors. He brings to its councils a practical experience that is without parallel in depth and breadth in Woolworth's history. He began his career with Woolworth's as a "learner" in the first Brooklyn store in 1897.

In 1909, Mr. Miller was one of the three men selected by F. W. Woolworth to pioneer F. W. Woolworth & Co., Limited (England). He was a Director of that company from its inception.

Recalled in 1920 to the United States, Mr. Miller was elected a Director, member of the Executive Committee and Vice-President of F. W. Woolworth Co. In 1923, he was elected Treasurer, and in 1932, President. His retirement in 1935 was occasioned by the 60-year compulsory retirement rule then in effect.

Mr. Miller held the office of President during the most difficult years of the Great Depression. It was during his administration that the 10¢ limit on the selling price was abolished.

Byron D. Miller, who was born in Elizabeth, Columbia County, New York, on December 30, 1875, now makes his home in Portland, Maine.

Fourth President and second Chairman of the Board, Charles W. Deyo was the first man in Woolworth's history to hold both posts. He was also the only President coming from S. H. Knox & Co.

Born in New Paltz, Ulster County, New York, on October 15, 1880, Mr. Deyo began his career on June 2, 1902, as assistant stockman in the London, Ontario, store of S. H. Knox.

Mr. Deyo rapidly moved up through the District Office organization, arriving at the Executive Office in 1929. Elected a member of the Board of Directors in 1930 and a Vice-President in 1932, Mr. Deyo championed the present policy of offering a wide range of merchandise without respect to arbitrary maximum prices.

C. W. Deyo led F. W. Woolworth Co. through World War II. Elected to the Presidency in 1936, he left that office in June, 1946. Meanwhile, sales had increased from $290 millions to $477 millions. Mr. Deyo, who succeeded C. S. Woolworth as Chairman of the Board in 1944, retired in 1950.

Charles W. Deyo was Honorary Chairman of the Board until his death on December 18, 1952.

The administration of Alfred L. Cornwell, President since 1946 and in addition Chairman of the Board since 1951, has been marked by the greatest growth in Woolworth's history. Annual sales have risen in this period from $477 millions to more than $700 millions.

The capital outlay for the modernization and improvement program initiated at the close of World War II will total, by the end of *Woolworth's First 75 Years*, approximately $175 millions.

The Amended Retirement Plan for Woolworth's employees, put into effect in 1946 after approval by the stockholders, is another Woolworth milestone.

Alfred L. Cornwell was born in Pulaski, New York, on January 5, 1884. He entered Woolworth's service as a "learner" in Worcester, Massachusetts, in January, 1905. By 1926, Mr. Cornwell was a member of the Board of Directors, and by 1930 a member of the Executive Committee. From 1932 to 1944 he was Vice-President and Treasurer. In 1944 he was elected Executive Vice-President.

As *Woolworth's First 75 Years* come to a close, Mr. Cornwell is in his forty-ninth consecutive year of service.

The pioneers and key executives lived to see F. W. Woolworth Co. take its place in the forefront of America's retail business world — but death then came to a number of them in shockingly quick succession. Carson C. Peck died April 29, 1915. S. H. Knox followed less than a month later, on May 16. C. C. Griswold, who had been appointed Peck's successor, also died January 27, 1916. W. H. Moore, F. W. Woolworth's first employer and lifelong friend, who had presided at the stockholders' meetings in 1914 and 1915, died suddenly on May 16, 1916, on the eve of that year's meeting.

F. W. Woolworth, who had been periodically in ill health since the spring of 1912, stepped back into the breach in 1915 to assume command again as Chairman of the Executive Committee. He successfully led his organization through the difficult days of World War I. Although his chosen role as buyer and later his British interests had taken him many times to Europe, he made his first trip to the Pacific Coast of the United States and Canada in the spring of 1916. He intended to visit his stores there incognito, as he had done in the East in his early days. Somewhat to his surprise, however, his journey was heralded by a fanfare of publicity and he was feted everywhere as a celebrity.

When F. W. Woolworth died on April 8, 1919, his organization consisted of 1,081 stores, located in every one of the 48 states and Canada, with annual sales of $119 millions.

The Fabulous Twenties

As F. W. Woolworth Co. entered the 1920s, C. S. Woolworth was Chairman of the Board, a new position. F. W. Woolworth's successor as President, Hubert T. Parson, was also Chairman of the Executive Committee. In 1920, Byron D. Miller returned from England, where he had helped found F. W. Woolworth & Co., Limited, and was elected a Director and Vice-President of F. W. Woolworth Co.

Despite the short but severe depression with which the 1920s began, the Company instituted two new employee benefits. For non-profit-sharing employees, an Employees' Benefit Fund was established in 1920. Administered by the Executive Committee, it was intended to aid needy employees. The fund was started with an appropriation of $100,000 and is now maintained at $300,000. It is wholly supported by the Company, through annual reimbursement of monies spent during the preceding year.

For profit-sharing employees, a Group Life Insurance Policy with Total Disability Provision was set up in 1922. The policyholder pays part of the premium, and Woolworth's the remainder. "Learners," heads

of food service departments and some supervisory employees also participate in a Group Insurance policy.

The next few years saw considerable progress in the foreign operations of F. W. Woolworth Co. In 1923, William L. Stephenson, the first Englishman employed when F. W. Woolworth & Co., Limited, was launched in England in 1909, became Managing Director of the company. He succeeded Fred M. Woolworth, who died January 26, 1923. Mr. Stephenson now is retired but remains a Director of F. W. Woolworth Co.

In 1924, Roy L. Creighton, a nephew of F. W. Woolworth, headed a group that started F. W. Woolworth Co. operations in Cuba. Two years later, R. H. Strongman was sent to Germany to launch F. W. Woolworth Co., G. m. b. H., there. The first German store was opened in Bremen in 1927.

The Company continued to prosper in America as well. F. W. Woolworth Co. ended the fabulous decade of the 1920s with 1,825 stores throughout the United States, Canada and Cuba, with sales in 1929 of $303 millions. Sales had more than doubled in ten years! The 1929 record was a high-water mark that stood until 1937.

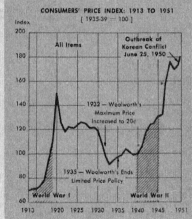

CONSUMERS' PRICE INDEX: 1913 TO 1951
[1935-39 — 100]

* Estimates of World War II and Postwar understatement by the index were not included. See Monthly Labor Review for March 1947.

Adapted from Fig. XV, Statistical Abstract of the United States 1952.

MINNEAPOLIS, 1937   FIFTH AVENUE, NEW YORK, 1939

With the inauguration of Woolworth's new merchandising policies in 1935, emphasis shifted from the number of stores to stores of greater size, consistent with the expansion of merchandise lines and with the greater sales potential. Before this expansion and improvement program was interrupted by the onset of World War II, stores like those pictured had been opened.

New Policy, New Expansion

Like the 1920s, the 1930s opened with a depression. Unlike the earlier one this economic "bust" not only persisted but eventually engulfed the world. The dark cloud of depression had its silver lining for Woolworth's, however, for it brought about a significant and far-reaching change in basic price and merchandising policy.

The first step leading to the change followed a report of current market conditions and buying opportunities made by C. W. Deyo, Supervisor of Buying, to the Board of Directors at the meeting of January 18, 1932.

At the conclusion of his report, it was recommended that Woolworth adopt a 20¢ price range.

The recommendation was unanimously approved. The reasoning proved sound, for the same forces that had been at work when F. W. Woolworth first went into business were again operating in 1932. Falling prices were opening up new vistas of variety and value to Woolworth's buyers, and it was proposed to take advantage of them.

On June 8, 1932, Byron D. Miller became President of F. W. Woolworth Co. and C. W. Deyo became a member of the Executive Committee. Miller succeeded H. T. Parson.

On November 13, 1935, the Board of Directors adopted officially the present policy of offering the public variety and value in merchandising without respect to arbitrary top selling price.

The timeliness of these changes in policy is indicated in the accompanying graph.

The new policy had enormously important and widespread effects on the whole pattern of the Company's store operations. Greatly expanded lines of merchandise – bigger items, made possible by higher price tags – required larger stores with improved appointments. The necessary change in the character of the store, in turn, opened up new potential sites for development.

Byron D. Miller, having reached his sixtieth birthday in December, 1935, retired as President. He was succeeded by C. W. Deyo. The new administration immediately launched a program of store enlargement, expansion and modernization reminiscent of F. W. Woolworth's own great programs. New, large stores were opened in impressive numbers in metropolitan centers. Other stores of all sizes, in widespread locations, were enlarged and modernized. Emphasis shifted from the *number* of stores to stores of greater size, consistent with the expansion of merchandise lines and with the greater sales potential.

To accelerate the expansion program, an issue of $10,000,000 debentures was sold in 1937. This loan was retired in 1940, with part of the proceeds of a new issue of $22,000,000 debentures. The onset of defense production, followed by World War II, forced temporary abandonment of the program. The debentures were therefore retired, $5,000,000 in 1942, the remainder in 1946.

The loss, through death, of Woolworth's pioneers

continued in the 1930s. Earle Perry Charlton died November 30, 1930. Illness forced Fred M. Kirby to resign from the Board of Directors and Executive Committee in 1938. He died October 16, 1940 and was succeeded on the Board by his son, Allan P. Kirby. Hubert T. Parson retired as a Director in 1938, and his death followed July 9, 1940.

F. W. Woolworth Co. weathered the economic storms of the 1930s with enviable stability. True, 1930 sales of $289 millions were less than the previous year for the first time since 1883, and sales continued to decline to a low of $250 millions in 1932. But they then turned up, and the decade closed with 1939 sales of $319 millions, a new high. Dividends were maintained at $2.40 throughout the 1930s, and even an extra $2 dividend was paid in 1931 as a result of liquidating part of the investment in the English company to help make possible a change from "private" to "public" ownership of that company. The Miller-Deyo-Cornwell management could take justifiable pride in the accomplishments of this trying decade.

The Troubled Forties

The effects of war — including the threat of war and the aftermath of war — marked Woolworth's operations during the 1940s. To deal with attendant problems, C. W. Deyo and A. L. Cornwell continued to complement and supplement each other. Upon the resignation of C. S. Woolworth as Chairman of the Board in 1944, Deyo was elected to that post, and continued in office as President. Cornwell was elected to the newly created position of Executive Vice-President. Cornwell succeeded Deyo as President in 1946, the latter continuing as Chairman of the Board.

On January 7, 1947, Charles Sumner Woolworth, the last surviving Founder, passed away.

Almost half the male employees of F. W. Woolworth Co. entered the armed services in World War II, and many of the female employees as well. The Company's service flag was emblazoned at war's end with 5,848 stars. Of these, 119 were Gold. Most of the positions vacated by the male employees had to be filled by women. Women not only managed more than 500 stores by the time the war was over, but filled many other important posts as well. Many of these women have remained as managers and some have advanced to supervisory positions. On the other hand, none of the men and women in service were permanently displaced. Many employees on military leave returned to better jobs than they had left, thanks to the expansion of business immediately after hostilities ceased.

One of the major tasks facing Woolworth's man-

SAN FRANCISCO, CALIFORNIA

agement at the end of the war was the retraining of these thousands of employees after an absence of years. Another was to try to resume the expansion and improvement program for stores which had been interrupted by the war. From 1941 through 1946, substantial reserves had been accumulated for this very purpose. Even with money available, however, the program was restricted first by actual shortages of needed materials and then by priorities covering materials that were not in sufficient supply.

Dividends, reduced during the war years to $1.60 per annum, have been at the annual rate of $2.00, plus a 50¢ extra, since 1947. The decade closed with sales in 1949 of $616 millions.

New Base for Progress

The problems of the 1940s recurred, in only slightly lessened degree, during the last three of Woolworth's First 75 Years. The Korean war erupted in June,

1950. The tremendous job of retraining and re-assigning returning World War II veterans had hardly been completed when large numbers of men again were called into service. This time it was again the ranks of the "learners" that were hardest hit, thinning out temporarily the reserves of management man-power necessary to expanding, efficient operations. At the same time, the program of store expansion and improvement, which had just been resumed, again was checked.

A. L. Cornwell succeeded C. W. Deyo as Chairman of the Board on January 1, 1951, retaining the office of President. Deyo was Honorary Chairman of the Board until his death on December 18, 1952. On January 1, 1953, J. T. Leftwich became Executive Vice-President. Leftwich had begun his career with Wool-worth's as an accountant in the Chicago District Office in 1913. He was named Assistant Secretary in 1925, Assistant Treasurer in 1932, Comptroller in 1947, Secretary in 1949, Vice-President and Trea-surer in 1952.

As *Woolworth's First 75 Years* come to a close, the Company can look backward with pride and forward with confident anticipation. Sales in 1952 for the first time in history passed the $700 million mark. With Korean hostilities at an end, the store expansion and improvement program is again under way.

In the pages that follow, the roles that all groups play in carrying forward the business of F. W. Wool-worth Co. are more fully discussed.

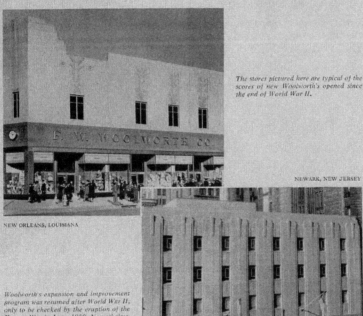

The stores pictured here are typical of the scores of new Woolworth's opened since the end of World War II.

NEWARK, NEW JERSEY

NEW ORLEANS, LOUISIANA

Woolworth's expansion and improvement program was resumed after World War II, only to be checked by the eruption of the Korean War in June, 1950. Nevertheless, the total investment in new and improved Woolworth stores in the period 1946-1954 will approximate $175 millions — the largest aggregate for any similar period in the Company's history.

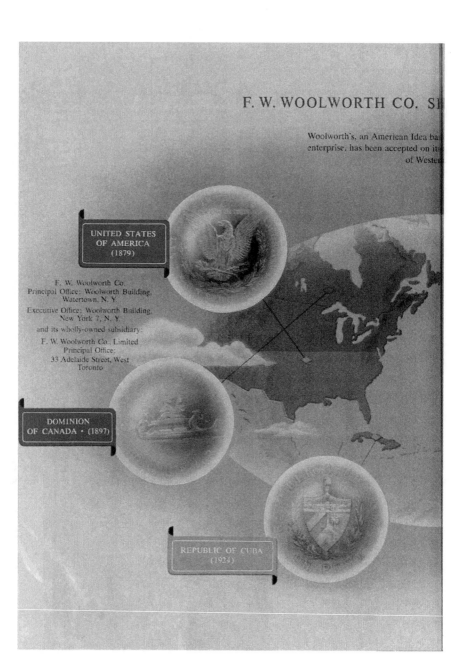

F. W. WOOLWORTH CO. S[

Woolworth's, an American Idea ba[
enterprise, has been accepted on it[
of Wester[

**UNITED STATES
OF AMERICA
(1879)**

F. W. Woolworth Co.
Principal Office: Woolworth Building,
Watertown, N. Y.

Executive Office: Woolworth Building,
New York 7, N. Y.

and its wholly-owned subsidiary:

F. W. Woolworth Co., Limited
Principal Office:
33 Adelaide Street, West
Toronto

**DOMINION
OF CANADA · (1897)**

**REPUBLIC OF CUBA
(1924)**

on the American Ideal of private
rits by other progressive peoples
ulture.

BRITISH ISLES
(1909)

F. W. Woolworth Co.
owns majority stock interest in:
F. W. Woolworth & Co., Limited
Principal Office: 1/5 New Bond Street,
London, W. 1.

and its wholly-owned subsidiary

F. W. Woolworth & Co., Limited (Eire)
Principal Office: Henry Street, Dublin

EIRE · (1914)

GERMANY · (1927)

F. W. Woolworth Co., G. m. b. H.,
Principal Office: Berlin
Executive Office: Frankfurt

PEOPLE
make
WOOLWORTH'S

Woolworth's owes its success not to industrial efficiency nor production capacity, but to individual human beings.

Unlike many other business giants, F. W. Woolworth Co. owns no mines or natural resources, no factories, and only the irreducible minimum of real estate properties which might come under the heading of "plant." The Company's greatest asset is *people*.

The very casualness with which F. W. Woolworth opened and closed his stores in his earlier days indicates that he regarded physical locations as simply soulless shells to house merchandise and offer it for sale. His regard for *people* was drastically different. *People*, as customers, dictated his every move; and *people*, as managers and friends, formed the nucleus around which his organization grew and prospered.

People have remained equally important in Woolworth's operations ever since.

A person with full freedom of economic choice walks into an F. W. Woolworth Co. store and makes a purchase. Without this simple act, the whole vast corporate structure is meaningless.

The item the customer purchases was where she wanted it, when she wanted it, only because of buyers, stock boys, display help, and the store manager. A sales girl takes the customer's money and wraps the purchase.

From the store, a chain reaction is set in motion and continued by still more people.

A large part of the price the customer pays the sales girl stays in the community — to pay wages, rents, taxes, transportation, and services of all kinds. A still larger part of what remains goes to the supplier of the item purchased. He, in turn, passes the money back to *his* suppliers: manufacturers, farmers and producers of basic raw materials.

The small portion of the money that is left is already earmarked for other *people*: for the salaries of managers, buyers and other administrative personnel; for Uncle Sam, in the form of Federal income tax; for the builders and suppliers of *future* Woolworth stores, in the form of retained earnings; and finally, for the stockholders in the form of dividends. Many stockholders, in turn, are educational and welfare institutions representing still other thousands of *people*.

Let's take a closer look, in the following pages, at the way these people operate, and cooperate, to make Woolworth's what it is today.

34

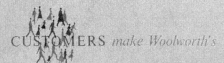

CUSTOMERS *make Woolworth's*

Woolworth's has no average or typical customer. Every person who enters a Woolworth store is an individual human entity with his own tastes and preferences, free to pick and choose, reject or purchase.

Realization of this fact has dictated the basic principle to which Woolworth's has adhered for 75 years: Customers *will* be served — and Woolworth's will serve them! Following this principle has led, paradoxically, to an almost infinite flexibility in actual operations. Policies arise spontaneously from the preferences of the customers, acting of their own individual free wills, at stores all over the United States, Canada and Cuba.

For example, customers' preferences, expressed in cash purchases, determine the actual selection of merchandise offered in all Woolworth stores. As 1954 opens, Woolworth customers have thousands of items of merchandise from which to choose. But not all of these items will be available at any one Woolworth's. The selections offered by the manager of each store are determined by the preferences of his particular customers by sales, and, in the case of new lines, by his own anticipation of customer demand, based on experience.

Furthermore, before the year ends, many new items will have been added, or major improvements made in existing items; and many old items will have

GROWTH IN NET SALES	
Calendar Year	Net Sales for Year
1912	$ 60,000,000
1918	100,000,000
1924	200,000,000
1929	300,000,000
1942	400,000,000
1946	500,000,000
1948	600,000,000
1952	700,000,000

been finally superseded. Every change will have been dictated by *customers*.

Similarly, Woolworth customers influence the kind of store in which they shop. Today's shoppers are educated, alert and sophisticated. They know style, materials, value. Consequently, their tastes are reflected in the store's equipment and appointments. Modern style and fashion are combined with the established sturdiness that has come to be associated with Woolworth's. The shopper's own intelligence is

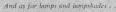

Thread? Woolworth's has it, and has it handy!   And as for lamps and lampshades . . .

Cleveland, Tennessee (above), and Cleveland, Ohio (right), each has its own Woolworth's, with store and stock adapted to its needs, as expressed by customer demand.

Smaller store (above) and larger store (right) each affords the store layout and lines of merchandise indicated by consumer preferences.

reflected also in the higher type of personnel serving in Woolworth stores each passing year.

Woolworth's depends upon its experience in anticipating customers' demands in order to offer new and timely merchandise. To keep well ahead of current consumer desires is a basic company policy. Hence, Woolworth's merchandise usually provides the answer to the question, from any member of the family, "What's new?"

How the policy is carried out is indicated for example in the candy department. Stocks are always fresh. In winter, when demand is at its peak, fine choco-lates from leading makers are featured. With the coming of summer, the cases are filled with seasonable items. Easter, Christmas, and other holidays are heralded with candy specialties characteristic of those seasons. At the same time, round-the-calendar staples are always on hand for the customer who wants them. So Woolworth's caters to these preferences; always will, as long as they prevail.

F. W. Woolworth recognized early in his business career that the *customer* is not always the *consumer* — and that where one member of the household acts as the purchasing agent for another, it is the ultimate

Woolworth's Lay Away Plan and Free Delivery Service, featured in the placards above, are popular Woolworth services.

The wanted ribbon, cut to the wanted length, is another service much appreciated by Woolworth's customers.

consumer who must be satisfied. For example, a wife might buy a toilet article for her husband or a toy for her child. Mr. Woolworth's personal conviction was that the sale was not finally consummated until the ultimate user was satisfied. Dating from his first store in Lancaster, he therefore instituted the privilege of return or refund for his customers. The policy has been continued and extended to every Woolworth store as it opened, up to the present time.

As customers' preferences continue to dictate changes in Woolworth policies, new ideas are constantly being introduced. For example, although Woolworth's cash policy is as old as the organization

Greeting cards that please both sender and recipient are available at Woolworth's the year round.

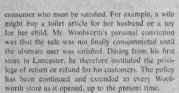

An extension of F. W. Woolworth's original concept of self-selection, the self-service idea is popular in many communities.

itself, F. W. Woolworth Co. for many years has offered a Lay Away Plan. Under this plan, a customer may select merchandise in advance of a season and make a small deposit to hold the item for delivery when desired.

Self-service stores are another innovation undergoing test and development in parts of the United States and Canada. At this point, it is difficult to say in what direction, and how far, self-service will finally go.

One thing is certain, however: customers will make the final decision in this and other matters — through the power of their purchases. For that is the way Woolworth's has operated during the whole of its first 75 years.

The freedom to choose from a great variety of goods to meet the needs and niceties of modern living, all in open display, all plainly priced — this freedom of self-selection is one of the greatest of the boons today's shopper owes to the pioneering of F. W. Woolworth and his Co-Founders. Today, Woolworth's brings the pleasurably profitable adventure of modern shopping to every member of every family in many communities.

EVERYBODY'S STORE

COMMUNITIES *make Woolworth's*

It is no coincidence that many an illustrator, when he sets out to portray "Main Street," shows a Woolworth store. Scarcely an adult today, when he recalls his home town, does not remember fondly his exciting excursions into the familiar variety store with the red-and-gold sign across the front. And, wherever he lives, chances are that Woolworth's is still his neighbor.

For, paradoxically, Woolworth, one of the world's largest retail companies, is essentially local in nature. Its entire business can be reduced to a local customer making an individual purchase in a local store. And almost every aspect of that store, from the sales transaction itself all the way back to the very inception of the establishment, is *local*. Let us see, for a moment, just how Woolworth helps build *your* community.

Woolworth contributes to the prosperity of the communities in which it operates in many ways. Per-

haps the most important contribution to community prosperity is the availability in Woolworth stores of a great array of good quality merchandise, selected by expert buyers, and offered at a low price. Woolworth buyers are, in effect, purchasing agents for the consumer, and customers can have confidence that the merchandise available to them at Woolworth's represents the greatest value the market affords. This is a major contribution to community prosperity and a factor helping to create higher standards of living.

Other contributions to community prosperity consist of wage payments to Woolworth employees, purchases of goods from local sources of supply, patronage of local banks and utilities, payment of taxes and rentals paid to local landlords. Woolworth values its harmonious relationships with all the groups with which the Company comes into contact.

The growth of Woolworth has brought to the small

An example of Woolworth's adaptation to a rapidly growing community is this store in Houston, Texas.

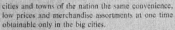
Suburban Seattle, Washington (above), and residential Princeton, New Jersey (right), each has a Woolworth's architecturally in harmony with the community.

cities and towns of the nation the same convenience, low prices and merchandise assortments at one time obtainable only in the big cities.

No longer is it necessary for the small town dweller to travel to the metropolitan shopping centers to fulfill wants and needs.

The store itself — that is, the physical plant — provides local benefits, too. Planning for community service begins long before it is opened. Convenience for shopper and employee, sanitation and accident prevention, permanence and ease of maintenance — all these are considered, in an effort to make the store one of the finest in the community.

Woolworth may, in some cases, buy land and erect a building, thus becoming a landlord to local business and professional men; it may lease the land, but build its own store. In the majority of cases, however, it rents its business property from a local landlord. Woolworth prides itself on its relationship with its landlords. Many leases in force today are direct successors of leases negotiated by F. W. Woolworth and the other Founders.

It is not surprising that the Company regularly receives invitations to open stores in new communities, and frequently gets expressions of appreciation from local people when new stores are opened or established stores are improved. Typical of many letters in Woolworth files is this one from a Chamber of Commerce president in a small town, who wrote: "We want you to know that your new store is considered a distinct asset to our community and we wish

to congratulate you on the progressive policies of your organization which have resulted in this improvement in the business development of this area."

But there is much more to sound and constructive community relations than the purely economic aspects of store operations. Woolworth managers are encouraged to take part in the civic life of their communities, to become active in service clubs and Chambers of Commerce, and to contribute financially to worthwhile community causes. In addition to Company contributions, managers and employees are encouraged to support established charities such as the Red Cross, Community Chest, and the various health funds.

Woolworth's regard for the local communities where it operates stems, in part at least, from the Founders themselves. F. W. Woolworth made Lancaster, site of his first successful store, his home until buying responsibilities forced him to move to New York. And even then he returned to erect in Lancaster the first building to bear his name. C. S. Woolworth in Scranton, F. M. Kirby in Wilkes-Barre, S. H. Knox in Buffalo, E. P. Charlton in Fall River — each of these Founders remained a lifelong local citizen and resident of the town that had given him his start.

In short, when Woolworth comes to a city, town or shopping center, it brings with it a sense of civic responsibility. It comes to stay, to contribute to the community, and add stability to the area. It realizes truly and humbly that it can continue to grow only insofar as it continues to *serve.*

STORE MANAGERS *make Woolworth's*

The basic operating unit of F. W. Woolworth Co. is the individual store. Therefore, upon the manager of the store — singly and collectively — rests the basic responsibility for the success of the entire organization.

The importance of the store manager is historic. F. W. Woolworth and the other Founders — C. S. Woolworth, F. M. Kirby, S. H. Knox, E. P. Charlton and W. H. Moore — all were store managers at the start. And to build their respective businesses, which formed F. W. Woolworth Co., each of the Founders had to train men to manage stores.

By direct lineal descent, the process continues to the present time. Every store manager starts his career as a "learner" — even as the Founders did. And the store manager is responsible for training other "learners" to carry on.

The importance of the store manager is organizational. From him and his peers is drawn every executive to fill an opening in the District and Executive Offices of F. W. Woolworth Co. Every elected officer in the history of the Company has come up through the organization, and those in merchandising operations at all levels gained their experience first as "learners" and then as store managers. Thus the store managers of today are indispensable as the source of the new management talent for the Woolworth's of tomorrow.

The importance of the store manager is also implicit in his day-to-day responsibilities, as he handles effectively the many details of his position.

He is responsible, first of all, to his customers. He must be constantly abreast of their preferences. From personal observation, from reports of his sales girls

In Bridgeport, Connecticut, as in hundreds of other communities, the Woolworth manager fosters worthwhile community programs.

and floor staff, he must be aware of current demands. From his own judgment and knowledge, he must decide what *new* lines, and in what assortment and quantity, he will add to his present stock. When new merchandise is received, the store manager must then instruct his staff in its values and the best way to display it — keeping the customer always in mind.

He is also responsible to his employees. Only through them does the store manager do business with his customers. He must employ, train and assign each employee to his or her job. He advances the more promising persons to better jobs as their skills increase. By developing an efficient, loyal and helpful sales and operating staff, he develops the means to build his store's business and enhance its value to his customers.

The store manager is responsible to the community. As an important merchant in his city and town, the Woolworth store manager is encouraged to participate in civic affairs as a privilege rather than an obligation. He is also assigned the duty of contributing to worthwhile civic projects from a budget specifically for that purpose. He alone is the judge of which needs are most worthwhile. As a rule, however, Community Chest and other established welfare activities are favored.

Finally, the store manager is responsible to F. W. Woolworth Co. itself. He must cope with competition. He recruits his employees in a competitive market. He makes sure his staff is well-trained and courteous. Above all, he must compete with other stores in merchandise, prices and merchandising methods.

He is responsible to F. W. Woolworth Co. for the kind of reputation the Company enjoys in his community. Behind him, he has the advantage of the good will that Woolworth has developed over the years in countless other communities, together with sound policies and principles to guide him in the same paths. Beyond this point, however, he is independently and completely accountable for the attitude that his fellow citizens in his own area have toward the Woolworth organization.

As a "learner" advances to assistant manager and finally to store manager, he becomes eligible to work on a profit-sharing arrangement. Thus he has the unusual prospect of entering into an employment contract that places no maximum on his earnings. Before him, he has the example of present and past senior executives of Woolworth's who advanced through the same experience.

Woolworth's store manager today is the key not only to the present but to the future as well.

43

 **EMPLOYEES** *make Woolworth's*

People make Woolworth's. But of all the groups of people who contribute to the successful operations of the Company, Woolworth's own employees are, of course, the most important.

Customers buy from Woolworth's. Suppliers furnish goods; farmers, crops. Stockholders support the management. But Woolworth's own people are the basic, essential group that brings all other groups into their proper focus. Theirs is the ultimate responsibility for all good will, all success.

F. W. Woolworth Co. provides employment to over 93,000 men and women in the United States, Canada and Cuba.

All sales girls and operating staff employees of a Woolworth store are under the direct jurisdiction of the store manager. His is the entire responsibility, to hire, train and supervise the individuals who work with him.

Each store manager, in turn, is responsible to the manager of his District. Woolworth's has 12 geographical Districts in the United States, Canada and Cuba. In addition, the District Manager has a staff of his own, under his direct jurisdiction. Among the staff are Superintendents of Stores, who are all former store managers themselves. They pay regular visits to stores under their supervision, on behalf of the District Manager, to render assistance on any problem.

The District Manager also has a merchandising staff that serves as a link between the stores and the

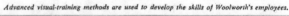
Advanced visual-training methods are used to develop the skills of Woolworth's employees.

Intervals of rest and recreation bring welcome breaks in the busy day of the Woolworth employee.

Executive Office buyers. Finally, he has an accounting staff that handles payment of all invoices for stores and maintains centralized records.

The District Managers operate under the jurisdiction of the Executive Office in New York. The Executive Committee and the Board of Directors make final decisions on policy.

Whether an employee works in a store, in a District Office or the Executive Office; whether he works on a salary or a profit-sharing basis; whether he is a stock boy or Chairman of the Board—every employee participates equally in Woolworth's program of paid vacations and holidays, in recognition of service, and in the Pension Plan.

Upon completion of six months' continuous employment, the new employee is entitled to a vacation of one week; after one full year, to two weeks; and after five years, to three weeks. All vacations and holidays are, of course, with pay.

After 25 years of continuous service, each employee receives a scroll and an appropriate gift.

Every employee becomes eligible for the Pension Plan when he or she attains the age of 35 or has five years' continuous service, whichever occurs later. Within 15 years of continuous service after the age of 35, the employee retains full credit for all pensions provided by the Company. Thus the employee usually acquires an irrevocable vested interest in the Pension Plan by age 50.

Certain other benefits are available to salaried employees, but not to profit-sharing personnel. Salaried employees only are entitled to a Christmas bonus. An Employees' Benefit Fund for the needy is also limited to them.

The employment policies of F. W. Woolworth Co. go back to F. W. Woolworth himself. When he opened his first Utica store, he employed two local helpers. On opening his successful Lancaster store, he employed seven. Subsequently, in all other stores, his employees were residents of the communities served by the stores. They thus brought to local operation an invaluable knowledge of local tastes and preferences. It was through these people that the Woolworth organization was able to take root and become an integral part of the community. Woolworth himself instituted profit-sharing, minimum wages, vacations and holidays with pay, Christmas bonuses, and progressive promotion policies back in the nineteenth century. His successors continue and advance these policies.

Thus, the spirit of F. W. Woolworth has persisted to this day. Employees remain the base on which all operations are predicated.

45

BUYERS *make Woolworth's*

When a customer walks into a Woolworth store and purchases an article, he is exercising what the economists call "demand." To meet that demand, a Woolworth buyer must have, in turn, purchased the article from a supplier.

Just as the store manager, through his sales girl, is the point of contact with the customer, so the Woolworth buyer is the point of contact with the manufacturer. The store manager is sensitive to every change in taste or preference of consumers in his community. Similarly, the buyer is sensitive to potential consumer satisfaction in new products, new materials and in all changed and improved products available from suppliers.

Linking customer with supplier, and store manager with buyer, is Woolworth's merchandising organization. At its head is a Vice-President, located in the Executive Office.

Each District Office has a counterpart of this merchandising staff. District Merchandise Supervisors work with managers of all stores in the District on matters pertaining to sales promotion; they also link the store manager with the buyer in the Executive Office.

There are over thirty full-time buyers who are the active representatives of the consumer. Their responsibility is to provide merchandise that is in consumer demand — to see that every Woolworth customer can buy what he or she wants. But beyond this, the buyer has the responsibility to anticipate demands, to develop new items, and to work far ahead with the manufacturers who will supply these requirements.

He must be able to look ahead and sense consumer demand. He serves as consultant and adviser to the manufacturer to make sure that quality and value are built into the final product.

If sales indicate the new product is a success, it is "listed" as available to all Woolworth stores. The manufacturer may thus find himself with national distribution almost overnight.

Every Woolworth buyer began as a "learner" and worked his way up through store manager, Superintendent of Stores, District Office staff member, and finally to the Executive Office as a specialist in his current buying activity. His merchandising experience is unassailable at all levels. His success depends on his ability to meet the needs of the consumer.

In this regard, the career of every Woolworth buyer parallels that of F. W. Woolworth himself — who started as a "learner," advanced to store manager, and then assumed broader buying duties. Incidentally, his buying duties were the last he reluctantly delegated, and then only to Carson C. Peck, his ablest and most valued lieutenant.

It is a heritage of which today's Woolworth buyer may well be proud.

Four great regional warehouses help Woolworth's buyers to assemble and distribute vast quantities of merchandise with economy and dispatch. This one is in Chicago, Illinois.

Famous lines developed by Woolworth's buyers — for the student: "University"; for business: "Herald Square"; for correct social usage: "Fifth Avenue." For him: "Blue Banner" tools and "Westchester" hose; for her, "Woolco" notions and "Primrose" superfine nylons; for him and her; "Lord Madison" and "Lady Madison" wallets.

Woolworth's buyers are always alert for the new and the useful, like these smartly styled, serviceable wallets.

SUPPLIERS *make Woolworth's*

In 1912, F. W. Woolworth wrote: "The success of our organization may be attributed to a great buying power and ability to take advantage of all cash discounts, combined with economy in distribution."

Although he made the statement to bankers in connection with the original public offering of F. W. Woolworth Co. securities, it describes accurately the basis of Woolworth's relationship with its suppliers for 75 years.

Suppliers need someone to *buy* their products and *distribute* them to the ultimate consumers. Woolworth's fills this need ideally, because it exists only to perform precisely those two functions. Woolworth's does not engage in manufacturing. On the other hand,

Enterprising and cooperative suppliers have helped Woolworth's pioneer consumer markets for articles of all kinds, made from non-inflammable and non-toxic plastics. These plastic toys are on sale in Woolworth's the year round.

Wool, a basic agricultural staple, is processed by Woolworth's suppliers into many useful forms.

by selling a wide range of products through widely situated stores, Woolworth's offers the supplier a more effective link with the consumer than he could possibly hope to develop by building his own distribution system.

As F. W. Woolworth's statement sets forth so clearly, the Company offers other advantages to suppliers as well. It buys in large quantities. This lowers the manufacturer's sales costs and assures him of a pay-out on his investments in raw materials and machinery. Woolworth's also pays cash.

Woolworth's suppliers, for their part, have been gratifyingly cooperative. They have added still further to the Company's own inherent economy of distribution. For example, many have opened regional warehouses to serve Woolworth's along with other customers. Some have gone a step farther and built manufacturing plants in outlying areas strategically located with regard to Woolworth's facilities.

Besides adding to the efficiency of distribution, these moves have served to spread the impact of Woolworth's vast buying power to countless additional communities. Direct suppliers of Woolworth's number a little over 6,000. But the Company's purchasing power permeates the whole industrial and agricultural economy of the country.

As a result of Woolworth's harmonious relations with its suppliers over the years, many of the buying connections that exist today were actually initiated personally by F. W. Woolworth in the 1880s. These include the importer who first supplied him with tinseled Christmas tree ornaments, and the pottery and glass manufacturers who supplied him with his first line of this type of merchandise. Economic conditions change and the terms of agreement change, but the basic supplier-seller relationship has remained active and mutually profitable.

After all, F. W. Woolworth Co. and its suppliers are in a kind of partnership to supply and please the customer. Perhaps the most priceless asset which Woolworth's contributes to this partnership is the knowledge, based on 75 years' experience, of what the customer wants to buy.

This knowledge is available to the *potential* supplier as well. Today, as it has throughout its history, Woolworth's offers a warm welcome to anyone with a new product, regardless of his experience or lack of experience with consumer markets. This welcome extends not only to the manufacturer with a new article which he thinks might interest the public, but also to the owner of manufacturing equipment adaptable to consumer articles, who is seeking a new line to turn out. Naturally, customers are always the final judges as to whether or not a new product is suitable for the consumer market. But drawing on their own years of merchandising experience, Woolworth's buyers help the manufacturer avoid many a pitfall.

To its customers, Woolworth's says: "Shop Woolworth's *first!*" Similarly, to all suppliers, Woolworth's issues the invitation: *"Try Woolworth's first!"*

49

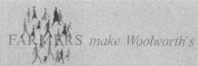

FARMERS *make Woolworth's*

F. W. Woolworth was a farmer first and a store-keeper second. All the Founders of Woolworth's were born on farms or in rural communities. And this background has left its indelible stamp upon the organization today. F. W. Woolworth Co. has a special and high regard for the farmer—first, as its most important single supplier; second, as a valued customer; and third, as a friend.

The public probably does not think of Woolworth's as one of the nation's largest purveyors of food service. Yet that is exactly what it is. Almost a thousand Woolworth stores, or nearly half of all stores in the U. S., Canada and Cuba, have a food service department—ranging from a counter offering a selection of hot and cold meals to a snack bar, beverage bar, or bake shop. Some of the larger stores have all these services. Whether food service is to be offered and in what form is determined—as in the case of all Woolworth's operations—by the needs of the customers.

In quality, quantity and price, a plate luncheon, a sandwich or a soda purchased in one Woolworth store is identical to the same item in any other Woolworth's. The menus are varied, however, to conform to local tastes. Wherever Woolworth food service is offered, however, its level of cleanliness and sanitation sets the standard for the community.

Organizationally, the food service department parallels the various merchandising departments of a Woolworth store. The sole difference is that the food service department *prepares* its own products. The merchandise departments buy and sell; the food service department buys, *prepares* and sells.

The food service department of every Woolworth store has its own manager who is responsible to the store manager. The food service manager requisitions materials and supplies mostly from local sources.

Each District Office has its own food service staff paralleling its merchandising staff. There is also an Executive Office staff which handles the purchasing, in quantity, of all finished, processed or semi-processed foodstuffs marketed on a national basis in nearly 1,000 food service departments.

As might be expected, the overwhelming majority of the members of the supervisory staff of Woolworth's food service department are women. Women are adaptable to this branch of management, and many have found satisfying and remunerative careers in it.

This all means that Woolworth's is a big customer

Utah turkey is featured in this Salt Lake City store. Each of almost 1,000 Woolworth food service departments draws supplies of fresh produce from its own local farming community.

of the nation's farmers. Some idea of just how big can be gained from the partial listing, on this page, of farm products purchased in a typical year.

Woolworth's greatest service to farmers, as to other suppliers, lies in buying large quantities for cash. For the success of the farmer, like that of the manufacturer, depends on his finding a ready market for his goods. The farmer has the added disadvantage of his goods being perishable. A bumper crop, therefore, can be either a boon or a disaster, depending on how soon it is sold and started on its way to the consumer.

That's where Woolworth's comes in. It is a ready buyer for many surplus crops. If there is a surplus of raisins, for example, then raisin custards and raisin sauces are likely to appear on Woolworth menus, and raisin pies and raisin cakes will suddenly appear on Woolworth bake shop counters. The same applies to many other crops.

At least once, Woolworth's cooperation with farmers to market a surplus crop played a dominant part

From farmer to consumer: Woolworth's bake goods are never more than hours old, and usually are minutes fresh!

FOOD PURCHASES
In a recent typical year

Beef	4,000,000 pounds
Ham	1,500,000 pounds
Pork, other than ham	2,000,000 pounds
Poultry	4,000,000 pounds
Eggs, fresh and frozen	3,000,000 pounds
Apples, fresh and canned	2,000,000 pounds
Oranges	300,000 cases
Fresh Milk	$4,000,000
Ice Cream	2,500,000 gallons
Butter	1,000,000 pounds
Potatoes	15,000,000 pounds
Flour	5,000,000 pounds

in changing the nation's eating customs. The crop was turkeys, which were in surplus supply years ago. Turkey growers' and marketers' associations sought the Company's cooperation – and received it. Turkey, normally a holiday meat, was added to regular daily menus of food service counters, with special displays and promotion. Customers were delighted with the idea, and their demand continued at such a level that turkey became a staple item. Dating largely from this venture, turkey has changed from a holiday bird to a feature dinner dish in most American homes and restaurants. Woolworth's part in bringing the change about is voluntarily attested by the growers themselves.

Similarly, Woolworth's cooperates with other growers' associations and other agricultural groups in special sales promotion programs. Every June, stores across the country carry a display in behalf of the dairy industry, and June menus feature dishes using milk and dairy products. At other seasons, the Company cooperates with cotton growers, wool growers and others.

Woolworth's also values the farmer as a customer, and tries to serve him accordingly. F. W. Woolworth himself, no doubt partially because of his own farm background, always preferred to locate his stores in small towns which served as shopping centers for surrounding farm country. Having decided that the farmer would be one of his principal customer groups, he then tried to reach as many farmers as possible by spreading Woolworth stores over as wide a geographical area as possible, rather than concentrating in population centers. Still with the farmer in mind, he stocked his stores with the widest possible variety of merchandise, appealing to all ages, with the idea of bringing to rural areas the identical articles available in the largest cities.

Finally, Woolworth's values the farmer as a friend. As a regular policy, the Company supports 4-H Clubs, Future Farmers of America, Future Homemakers of America and similar groups in local communities. It also participates as opportunity presents itself in suitable programs of all recognized farm organizations. F. W. Woolworth Co. has taken its place beside the farmer in working toward a better America.

51

CAREER OPPORTUNITIES *make Woolworth's*

As Woolworth's enters its seventy-fifth year, it continues to offer attractive opportunities to promising young men and women. The Company has grown phenomenally and is continuing to grow. And it is looking for young people who are interested in making retailing their career.

Today's "learners" are the foundation on which tomorrow's Woolworth's will be built. Every vacancy in the Woolworth organization is filled, as a matter of fixed policy, from within. Store managers are selected from the ranks of the learners, and all other executive posts are filled from the ranks of the store managers. Some idea of the scope and range of opportunity is indicated by the number of executive positions that exist today: 53 executives including buyers in the Executive Office; 12 District Managers with approximately 300 other executives in District Offices; and nearly 2,000 store managers.

High school and college graduates are given preference in the selection of candidates for the "learners" training program, but any earnest young man who feels he can qualify is invited to make application.

The "learner" facing his first day in the Woolworth organization is in a far different situation than was the Company's first career man, Frank W. Woolworth himself, as he faced *his* first day. F. W. Woolworth served his apprenticeship without pay. Today's learner not only receives a good starting salary, but regular increases commensurate with his progress.

The tradition of individual, personal training of candidates for managerial positions is as old as Woolworth's. Here an aspiring "learner" takes on larger responsibilities under the guidance of a successful manager.

Women are important to the present operation and future growth of Woolworth's. The food service department affords many interesting and challenging career opportunities for capable women.

The present "learners" training program runs from 36 to 48 months or longer, depending on the ability of the individual and circumstances. It is designed to develop the learner into a trained merchant ready to take over management of a store. The training program is divided into four periods, running from 9 to 12 months each. The first period is devoted to stock-keeping and operation of the physical plant. The remaining three periods are devoted to merchandising, from the ordering of the stock to the sale over the counter, with full coverage of display, training of sales personnel, expense control, and every other phase of retail merchandising. It is the kind of on-the-job training that can't be obtained in any school, with a faculty made up of men who have developed and proved the Woolworth principles of operation.

As training progresses and the learner moves from store to store, he is upgraded to the Advanced Group, then to the Preferred Group, then to store manager.

Many opportunities are also open to young men with training and inclination toward the restaurant, real estate, construction, traffic, and financial functions of the Company. They may start either in a store or in a District Office, with ample chances for advancement.

Opportunities exist for young women as well as young men in F. W. Woolworth Co. To succeed, they need only bring to their work the same attitudes and abilities that are essential for the career man. Today, many Woolworth stores are managed by women, and women hold many other important and remunerative posts in the District and Executive Offices.

One of F. W. Woolworth's great qualities of genius was his skill in developing latent talents and managerial ability in the associates he chose. The executives of F. W. Woolworth Co. today take pride in carrying on the same tradition of mutual helpfulness.

53

CANADIANS *make Woolworth's*

With the celebration of *Woolworth's First 75 Years,* Canada's own Woolworth's marks its 57th anniversary. It was founded April 30, 1897, when S. H. Knox opened his first store in Toronto. Not long afterward, E. P. Charlton opened a store in Montreal.

Canada was quick to accept the idea of the variety store, and at the inception of F. W. Woolworth Co. in 1912, the Company had 31 stores in the Dominion. At the close of the present anniversary year, 170 Woolworth stores will be in operation in Canada, located in all provinces except Newfoundland.

The growth of Canada's own Woolworth's is but a reflection of the growth of the country itself. In a century that has been characterized by industrial development, the industrialization of Canada still stands out as a notable achievement. When Woolworth's opened in Canada at the close of the nineteenth century, Canada was primarily an agricultural nation. Today, although she remains an agricultural giant, Canada ranks among the great industrial nations of the world.

And her growth is probably only beginning. Blessed with an abundance of such vital natural resources as oil and uranium, Canada is generally regarded by authorities as one of the most promising economic frontiers.

F. W. Woolworth Co., Limited, of Canada is an integral part of F. W. Woolworth Co. It receives the

Entrance to the modern building which houses the Principal Office of F. W. Woolworth Co., Limited, in Toronto.

Some signs in stores in Quebec Province are in French, but dolls speak a language understood by little girls everywhere.

54

support and benefit of the total resources of the parent Company. At the same time, Woolworth's in Canada is entirely Canadian in operation. That is, it is managed and staffed by Canadians at all levels; all purchases are made in Canada; and all but a small percentage of goods sold are of Canadian origin. At all times the Canadian company is represented in the management of the parent Company by a Canadian member on the Board of Directors.

The employees of Canadian Woolworth's enjoy the same benefits and protections as those of the Company in the United States: vacations with pay, Christmas bonuses, participation in the Pension Plan, and eligibility for help from the Employees' Benefit Fund. Store managers and executive personnel at all levels are eligible for profit-sharing. They also enjoy the benefit of the Group Life Insurance and Disability Policy.

Woolworth stores in Canada are, in general, worthy representatives of the great country they serve. They have undergone the same evolution in policy and the same improvement in physical characteristics as their counterparts in the United States. As the economy of the Canadian nation continues to expand in the years ahead, F. W. Woolworth Co., Limited, will undoubtedly assume an even more prominent role in the Woolworth organization as a whole.

Woolworth's is justifiably proud to be a contributor, in small part at least, to Canada's emergence as the bulwark of the British Commonwealth of Nations and as a world power in her own right. Canada's Woolworth's is ready for the future.

Vancouver was pioneered for Woolworth's by E. P. Charlton a half-century ago.

S. H. Knox opened his first Canadian store in 1897. This store is its modern successor.

The BRITISH and IRISH *make Woolworth's*

"... I think a good penny and six pence store run by a live Yankee would create a sensation here. ..."

So wrote Frank W. Woolworth from England on his first visit there in 1890. The "live Yankee" whom Woolworth had in mind was himself, of course, and 19 years later he sailed for England to establish a British Woolworth company. He took with him Fred Moore Woolworth (a third cousin), B. D. Miller and S. R. Balfour. Upon his arrival in England, he hired an Englishman, young William Lawrence Stephenson. Stephenson had impressed Woolworth favorably on an earlier visit to England, when, as a junior clerk in an export firm, he proved helpful in the latter's buying ventures.

On July 23, 1909, F. W. Woolworth & Co., Limited, was incorporated in England as a "private limited" company. Capitalization of £50,250 was represented by 5,000 Preference (7%) shares at £10 per share, and 5,000 Ordinary shares at one shilling per share. This was the only investment ever made in British Woolworth's by F. W. Woolworth Co. From then on, in keeping with Woolworth's policy, all growth was from earnings alone.

This new Woolworth's serves Southsea, England.

Fred M. Woolworth was Chairman of the Board and Managing Director of F. W. Woolworth & Co., Limited, at its formation. B. D. Miller was a Director. He returned to the United States in 1920 to become Vice-President and, in 1932, President of F. W. Woolworth Co. S. R. Balfour, the other member of the British company, was soon forced to return to the United States due to ill health.

The first English store opened in Liverpool on November 6, 1909. As F. W. Woolworth had predicted in his letter nearly 20 years before, the "penny and six pence" idea was an immediate success. By 1914 a total of 44 Woolworth stores were operating in England, Scotland, Wales and what is now Eire and Northern Ireland. Except for a few trained men sent from the U. S. to replace Britons called to service when World War I broke out, F. W. Woolworth & Co., Limited, has employed and trained its own men for management. W. L. Stephenson became Chairman of the Board and Managing Director in 1923, when Fred M. Woolworth died.

Blackpool, England, on the Irish Sea, is the site of this great new Woolworth's.

Until 1931, F. W. Woolworth Co. owned 62 per cent of the Ordinary shares of F. W. Woolworth & Co., Limited. Then British Woolworth's, under Stephenson's leadership, changed its status from "private limited" to a "public" company. To make a public stock issue possible, holders of Ordinary shares yielded 15% of their holdings. This transaction reduced the interest of F. W. Woolworth Co. in the Ordinary shares of the British company to 52.7% and yielded a non-recurring profit of $9,977,452 — equal to 90 cents per share of the Common Stock of F. W. Woolworth Co.

F. W. Woolworth & Co., Limited, suffered grievously in World War II. Out of 766 stores operating when the war started, 26 in the largest cities were completely destroyed by enemy action, and 326 others were damaged. Nearly 2,500 male employees and large numbers of female employees left to serve in the National Service. Other women took over the management of hundreds of stores, and are to be commended for a job well done.

This store in Edinburgh is one of the many Woolworth's serving Scotland.

Belfast, in Northern Ireland, has been served by Woolworth's since 1914.

For a period of years after the cessation of hostilities, British Woolworth's was limited by government regulation to an annual expenditure of £10 per store for maintenance; and during a later period, to £100 per store. With the gradual easing of restrictions, the company looks forward to a rehabilitation program. New stores also are being opened, with the result that over 800 stores are now in operation.

F. W. Woolworth & Co., Limited, has a present authorized capitalization of £20,000,000 in the form of

£ 5,000,000 in 6% Cumulative Preference Stock

and

£15,000,000 in Ordinary Stock

The management of F. W. Woolworth & Co., Limited, is entirely British. It is headed by S. V. Swash, Chairman of the Board, W. J. Turner, Managing Director, and O. Hunter, Executive Director, all of whom have advanced through the ranks of the British Company. F. W. Woolworth Co. is represented on the board of F. W. Woolworth & Co., Limited, by J. T. Leftwich.

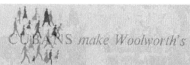

The Republic of Cuba has taken Woolworth's to its warm and friendly Latin heart. The Company's operations there are an excellent example of the flexibility and adaptability inherent in the intelligently managed variety store.

F. W. Woolworth Co. opened its first Cuban store on December 20, 1924, at the corner of San Rafael and Amistad Streets, in Havana. Today Cuba boasts eight Woolworth stores, which are supervised and operated as a branch of the parent company. With very few exceptions, all personnel employed by Woolworth's in Cuba has been recruited and trained there. All these employees enjoy benefits which conform to the customs and laws of the Republic of Cuba.

Variety and value in wanted merchandise are available to Woolworth's Cuban customers in the new Havana store.

food service departments have proved very popular in Cuba, with bake goods, especially cream-filled pastries, in great demand.

Woolworth's has always offered Cuban customers the same quality and variety of merchandise found in its United States stores. Wherever possible, Woolworth's features in its Cuban stores merchandise and products of Cuban origin, produced with Cuban labor.

In July, 1953 one of the largest and most beautiful Woolworth stores was reopened in Havana. The photographs on this page tell vividly Woolworth's progress in three decades in Cuba.

The food service department of Woolworth's new Havana store is as fine as any in the world.

Cuba's newest Woolworth's was reopened in Havana in 1953.

Woolworth's stores in Cuba introduced many staple lines that had been developed in the United States. It was necessary for the initial store to import ice cream, but the demand was so great Cuba soon developed her own ice cream industry. This experience was repeated with other products. Frankfurters and turkey dinners were two other food specialties that enjoyed immediate Cuban acceptance. Candy and

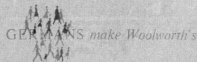

GERMANS *make Woolworth's*

In the autumn of 1926, the F. W. Woolworth Co. sent R. H. Strongman, a veteran executive and Director, to Germany to establish F. W. Woolworth Co. G. m. b. H.

Strongman became the German company's first Managing Director. Assistant Managing Director was Ivan W. Keffer, a Canadian who had begun his career in the Hamilton, Ontario, store of F. W. Woolworth Co., Limited, in 1912.

thriving Woolworth stores in operation. Of these, 70 were either destroyed or damaged during World War II. After V-E Day, Jahn and his staff immediately began to rebuild, drawing only upon the German company's own meager resources. Today 50 Woolworth stores are again serving communities in Western Germany, and the Company is in process of being rehabilitated comparable to pre-war standards.

The original capitalization of F. W. Woolworth Co.

A typical interior of a Woolworth store in Germany.

Among the management group accompanying these men was Rudolf Jahn, a German who had been trained in the Woolworth organization in America.

The first Woolworth store in Germany was opened July 30, 1927, in Bremen. Success was immediate and growth was rapid.

Ivan W. Keffer succeeded Strongman as Managing Director in 1933. Rudolf Jahn succeeded Keffer as Managing Director in January, 1939. Keffer returned to the Canadian organization and later joined the New York Executive Office staff, eventually becoming Executive Vice-President of F. W. Woolworth Co. He retired in 1953.

When the United States and Germany went to war in 1941, F. W. Woolworth Co. G. m. b. H. had 82

G. m. b. H., at its formation in 1926, was Rm 400,000. In 1954, after the losses of war and the reconstitution of Germany's monetary system, capitalization is Dm 16,000,000, of which 97% is owned by F. W. Woolworth Co. This investment is carried on the present balance sheet of F. W. Woolworth Co. at $1, having been written down in 1941, due to the war.

The loyalty and industry of Rudolf Jahn and the entire German organization deserve the highest commendation. Western Germany has been called "the showcase of democracy." If this is so, Woolworth's there should rate as a prime example of the American system of enterprise at work, under wholly German management.

Post-war Woolworth store in Bochum, Westphalia.

Stuttgart is the site of this new Woolworth store.

F. W. WOOLWORTH CO.

General Balance Sheet as of December 31, 1912

ASSETS

PROPERTY (Book Values):
Real Estate and Buildings ...... $ 1,474,567.37
Furniture and Fixtures 3,360,614.42
Lease Right 17,149.24

$ 4,851,991.03

GOODWILL 50,000,000.00
SECURITIES OWNED 665,929.44
MORTGAGE RECEIVABLE 29,000.00
CASH ON DEPOSIT TO PAY DIVIDEND 262,500.00

INVENTORY AND CURRENT ASSETS:
Inventory 8,626,841.36
Current Assets:
Cash on hand and on deposit ... 2,473,094.44
Notes and accounts receivable .. 76,000.88
Advance payments on goods in transit 83,584.81
Dividend accrued on securities owned 4,022.90
Proportion of surplus of F. W. Woolworth & Co., Ltd. applicable to dividends 84,992.86
Interest accrued 37.82

11,455,649.92

DEFERRED CHARGES TO OPERATIONS:
Alterations and improvements upon leased premises, to be written off during the terms of the various leases and organization expenses, to be written off during the next five years 1,614,547.29
Office and store supplies, Insurance, etc. 311,964.28

1,926,511.66

$69,187,492.74

CAPITAL AND LIABILITIES

CAPITAL STOCK:
Preferred, 150,000 shares par value, $100 each $15,000,000.00
Common, 200,000 shares par value, $100 each 50,000,000.00

$65,000,000.00

MORTGAGES PAYABLE 315,000.00

CURRENT LIABILITIES:
Accounts payable 61,080.39
Interest accrued 3,251.27
Taxes accrued 1,995.54

66,327.20

DIVIDEND ON PREFERRED STOCK PAYABLE JAN. 1, 1913 .. 262,500.00
RESERVE FOR DEPRECIATION OF FURNITURE AND FIXTURES 481,856.64
SURPLUS 3,061,708.90

$69,187,492.74

Income Account for the year ending December 31, 1912

NET SALES $66,387,763.78

NET INCOME 5,181,799.90

DIVIDENDS:
Preferred capital stock (7 per cent.) $1,050,000.00
Common capital stock (two dividends, 1 per cent. each) 1,000,000.00

2,050,000.00

BALANCE TO SURPLUS $3,364,799.90

F. W. Woolworth Co.,
280 Broadway,
New York City.

We certify that the foregoing Balance Sheet and related Income Account are true Exhibits of the accounts and that, in our opinion, they correctly set forth the financial condition of the Company as of December 31, 1912 and the results from operations for the period stated.

THE AUDIT COMPANY OF NEW YORK.

(Signed)   (Signed)
A. W. Tonning,   G. H. Rogers,
President.   *Secretary.*

New York,
February 14, 1913.

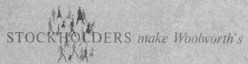

STOCKHOLDERS *make Woolworth's*

From the foregoing accounts of Woolworth's past history and present organization, a pattern emerges. We have seen, for example, that Woolworth's has built its management structure from within. Frank W. Woolworth's close associates in the Company were drawn largely from friends from his Watertown days. And later managers were promoted from the ranks of able and ambitious employees, spurred by the incentive of sharing in the net profits earned.

Growth from Within

In the same way, F. W. Woolworth Co. has grown financially entirely from within. In this regard, Woolworth's is certainly unusual, and probably unique. F. W. Woolworth started in business on February 22, 1879, owing $315.41, but by reinvesting his own earnings, he ended the year with a net worth of $1,516.60. Each of the other Founders of Woolworth's started in business on a similarly small investment – often in the form of a loan, and all of them prospered by the same means. It has been estimated that the aggregate net initial investments of all the Founders, on which F. W. Woolworth Co. is built, totaled less than $10,000! Except for this relatively insignificant amount, substantially all the capital of present-day Woolworth's has accrued from retaining and reinvesting part of the profits derived from sales. In short, F. W. Woolworth Co. is almost wholly consumer-financed.

The same pattern is evident in foreign operations. In both the British and German companies, F. W. Woolworth Co. provided only necessary initial capital – *and* key operating principles. The companies have grown to their present impressive size and importance solely through retaining and reinvesting profits, and through building their organizations from within.

Public Participation

Thus, as has been seen, when F. W. Woolworth Co. securities were offered to the public, it was by a Founder, or his representative, rather than by the Company. Every stockholder today is a direct successor of a Founder in ownership, and his capital went to an owner and not into the treasury of the corporation.

The Common Stock was listed on the New York Stock Exchange on June 26, 1912. The first dividend was paid to stockholders of record on August 1, 1912. The highest price at which the Common Stock had sold up to that time was $84 per share.

At first, only a few could participate as stockholders in F. W. Woolworth Co. Then, as more shares became available through stock dividends and split-ups, and through liquidation by original holders, more and more investors bid for the Common Stock. By 1929 the number of stockholders crossed the 10,000 mark. Today, 9,750,000 shares are outstanding, in the hands of over 88,000 stockholders.

F. W. Woolworth Co. has paid a dividend every year since its incorporation. Since 1947, dividends have been on an annual basis of $2.50 per share.

The Company's surplus has more than doubled in the past ten years – from $108 millions to $228 millions. Net working capital alone stands at more than $100 millions.

Fiscal Policy

The goal of Woolworth's fiscal policy can be stated in one word: *liquidity!* The Company's policy of paying cash has not only attracted desirable suppliers, but has been reflected in the net earnings. From time to time, short-term bank credit is used, usually for seasonal needs. When justified by prospects for increased sales volume and timely liquidation, and when the cost of money was low, longer-term borrowings have been made. The latest of these, authorized on May 13, 1953, by the Board of Directors, is a 20-year loan of $35 millions from the Equitable Life Assurance Society of the United States, at 3½% interest and on favorable terms.

Proved Principles

As *Woolworth's First 75 Years* draw to a close, the "original principles" set forth by F. W. Woolworth and his Co-Founders still guide the destinies of F. W. Woolworth Co. At their base is the principle of mutual interest and mutual respect in all relations between Woolworth's and those whose contributions make F. W. Woolworth Co. possible: the consumers . . . communities . . . landlords . . . suppliers . . . farmers . . . managers . . . employees . . . and stockholders.

Above all, it is the good will of these groups – particularly the customers, from whom all growth stems – that constitutes the true and enduring value of F. W. Woolworth Co.

61

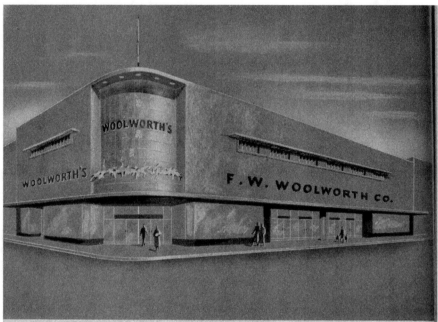

Preliminary sketch for Woolworth's in Honolulu, planned to be opened in 1954

STILL BUILDING
FOR TOMORROW

The world's first successful variety store was opened by F. W. Woolworth in Lancaster, Pennsylvania, June 21, 1879.

As the record shows, the success of the F. W. Woolworth Co. of today is a continuation and extension of that initial success.

Throughout *Woolworth's First 75 Years*, the Company's growth has come from the reinvestment in the business of a part of its own earnings. As resources permitted, Woolworth's has opened new stores in new markets. This policy continues.

Shown above is a preliminary sketch for a new Woolworth's planned for opening late in 1954. It will feature every modern facility for the convenience and comfort of both customers and employees. Located in downtown Honolulu, it will be Hawaii's first Woolworth's.

As the Founders did in the beginning, so their successors today are *still building for tomorrow*.

F. W. WOOLWORTH CO.

--------- *Officers* ---------

ALFRED L. CORNWELL
President and Chairman, Board of Directors

JAMES T. LEFTWICH
*Executive Vice-President
and Treasurer*

HARRY E. WILSON
*Comptroller and Assistant
Treasurer*

GEORGE F. TERPENNING
Vice-President

TROUSDALE BROWN
Secretary

HERBERT J. COOK
Vice-President

C. HOWARD LOVELL
*Assistant Secretary and
Assistant Treasurer*

CARSON C. PECK
Vice-President

JAMES R. WEBB
Assistant Treasurer

L. JAMES THRASHER
Vice-President

CARYL T. HALLDORSON
Assistant Secretary

RAYMOND E. WILLIAMS
Vice-President

THOMAS J. MULLEN
Assistant Secretary

--------- *Directors* ---------

RUSSELL D. CAMPBELL	*Manager, Canadian District*
HERBERT J. COOK	*Officer and Member of Executive Committee*
ALFRED L. CORNWELL	*Officer and Chairman of Executive Committee*
ALEXANDER R. GALLENKAMP	*Manager, Minneapolis District*
LEWIS H. GAUSE	*Manager, Manhattan District*
SAMUEL H. HUBER	*Dalton, Pa.*
IVAN W. KEFFER	*Toronto, Ont.*
ALLAN P. KIRBY	*President of Alleghany Corporation*
ROBERT C. KIRKWOOD	*Manager, Boston District*
SEYMOUR H. KNOX	*Chairman of Board, Marine Trust Company of Western New York*
JAMES T. LEFTWICH	*Officer and Member of Executive Committee*
BYRON D. MILLER	*Former President, Portland, Me.*
CARSON C. PECK	*Officer and Member of Executive Committee*
FREMONT C. PECK	*New York, N. Y.*
WALTER E. SAUNDERS	*Manager, Cleveland District*
MARTIN A. SCHENCK	*Attorney, Member of Firm, Davies, Hardy & Schenck*
WILLIAM E. SMITH	*Supervisor of Real Estate*
WILLIAM L. STEPHENSON	*Former Chairman, F. W. Woolworth & Co., Ltd., England*
JOHN E. STROMENGER	*Member of Executive Committee*
GEORGE F. TERPENNING	*Officer and Member of Executive Committee*
L. JAMES THRASHER	*Officer and Member of Executive Committee*
HARRY E. WARD	*Honorary Chairman of Board, Irving Trust Company, N. Y.*
RAYMOND E. WILLIAMS	*Officer and Member of Executive Committee*
RICHARD W. WOOLWORTH	*Salem Center, N. Y.*

January, 1954

F. W. WOOLWORTH CO.

Executive Office: WOOLWORTH BUILDING, NEW YORK 7, N. Y.
Principal Office: WOOLWORTH BUILDING, WATERTOWN, N. Y.

District Offices

ALBANY . . . . *State Bank Building, 75 State Street, Albany, N. Y.*

ATLANTA . . . . *Hurt Building, P. O. Box 1676, Atlanta, Ga.*

BOSTON . . . . *639 Massachusetts Avenue, Cambridge, Mass.*

CHICAGO . . . . *228 North La Salle Street, Chicago, Ill.*

CLEVELAND . . . . *1400 Leader Building, Cleveland, Ohio*

DENVER . . . . *1370 Pennsylvania Street, Denver, Colo.*

MANHATTAN . . . . *18th floor, Woolworth Building, New York, N. Y.*

MINNEAPOLIS . . . . *Midland Bank Building, Minneapolis, Minn.*

PHILADELPHIA . . . . . *123 South Broad Street, Philadelphia, Pa.*

ST. LOUIS . . . . *3663 Lindell Boulevard, St. Louis, Mo.*

SAN FRANCISCO . . . . *405 Montgomery Street, San Francisco, Calif.*

TORONTO . . . . *33 Adelaide Street, West, Toronto, Ontario, Canada*

DESIGNED AND PRINTED IN U.S.A. WILLIAM E. RUDGE'S SONS, NEW YORK

WOOLWORTH'S
FIRST 75 YEARS

1879   1954